Joe —

always gratefully,

Daniel

11/'07

NO BARS
TO MANHOOD

NO BARS
TO MANHOOD

by Daniel Berrigan

WIPF & STOCK · Eugene, Oregon

Acknowledgment is made to the following for permission to reprint their material:

CONTINUUM

"The Best of Times: The Worst of Times" from *Continuum*, Summer 1968. Reprinted by permission of *Continuum*.

THE CRITIC

"Exit the King and Crisis of America" from *The Critic*. Copyright © 1969 by The Thomas More Association. Reprinted by permission of *The Critic*.

JESUIT MISSION

"Pauperes Semper: A Non-Encyclical" from *Jesuit Mission* magazine.

KATALLAGETE

"Open Sesame: My Life and Good Times" from *Katallagete*. Reprinted by permission of *Katallagete*-Be Reconciled, the Journal of the Committee of Southern Churchmen.

MOTIVE

"Trial by Fire" from the February 1969 issue of *Motive* magazine. Copyright © 1969 by the Board of Education, United Methodist Church. Reprinted by permission of *Motive* magazine.

NATIONAL CATHOLIC REPORTER

"This Man Is Armed: The Cleaver of Eldridge" from March 19, 1969, issue of *National Catholic Reporter*. Reprinted by permission of *National Catholic Reporter*.

U. S. CATHOLIC

"Conscience, the Law, and Civil Disobedience" from July 1969 issue of *U. S. Catholic*. Reprinted by permission of The Claretian Publications.

Wipf and Stock Publishers
199 W 8th Ave, Suite 3
Eugene, OR 97401

No Bars to Manhood
A powerful, personal statement on radical confrontation
with contemporary society
By Berrigan, Daniel
Copyright©1970 by Berrigan, Daniel
ISBN 13: 978-1-55635-471-7
ISBN 10: 1-55635-471-1
Previously published by Doubleday, 1970

my father
Thomas Berrigan (1879–1969)
my brother
Thomas Merton (1915–1968)

SERIES FOREWORD

Daniel Berrigan is one of the most influential American Catholics of the twentieth century. A Jesuit priest, poet, and peacemaker, he has inspired countless people of faith and conscience to pursue the gospel vision of a world without war or nuclear weapons. Born in 1921, he entered the Society of Jesus in 1939, was ordained in 1952, and in 1957 published his first book of poetry, *Time Without Number*, which won the prestigious Lamont Poetry Award.

Since then Daniel Berrigan, my friend and Jesuit brother, has published over fifty books, including the award-winning play, *The Trial of the Catonsville Nine* (1970); an autobiography, *To Dwell in Peace* (1987); and many journals, essays, poetry collections, and scripture commentaries. Dan maintained close friend friendships with Thomas Merton and Dorothy Day. He also co-founded the Catholic Peace Fellowship and Clergy and Laity Concerned about Vietnam. But because of his early peace work, church authorities banished him to Latin America in 1966 and 1967. In early 1968, he traveled to Hanoi with Howard Zinn to experience firsthand the horrors of U.S. war-making and to rescue three U.S. soldiers who had been captured.

On May 19, 1968, with his brother Philip and other friends, he burned military draft files using homemade napalm in Catonsville, Maryland—an action which galvanized millions against the Vietnam war. For this creative nonviolence, Dan was tried, convicted, and sentenced to years in prison. In April of 1970, however, he went underground, eluding the FBI, and continued to draw widespread attention to his antiwar message. He was finally arrested in August, and imprisoned in Danbury, Connecticut until February 1972.

He continued to write and speak against war and nuclear weapons throughout the 70s. On September 9, 1980, both he and Philip participated in the first Plowshares Action, a protest at the General Electric Plant at King of Prussia, Pennsylvania. He faced ten years in prison, but was eventually sentenced to time served.

Since the early 1970s, Dan has lived in New York City with his Jesuit community. He continues to give lectures, conduct retreats, publish books of poetry and scripture study—and get arrested for his protests against war, injustice, and nuclear weapons. He remains a clear voice of resistance to war, gospel nonviolence, and peace for humanity.

Throughout his faithful, peacemaking life, Daniel Berrigan has consistently said no to every war, injustice, and weapon of violence. And with every no he accepts the cost. And he does not give up. Nominated many times for the Nobel Peace Prize, Dan often finds himself with friends before some judge and sitting on ice in some dismal holding cell. Such is the mark of a prophet, the sign of an apostle of peace.

"We have assumed the name of peacemakers," Dan writes in *No Bars to Manhood,*

> but we have been, by and large, unwilling to pay any significant price. And because we want the peace with half a heart and half a life and will, the war, of course, continues, because the waging of war, by its nature, is total—but the waging of peace, by our own cowardice, is partial. There is no peace because there are no peacemakers. There are no makers of peace because the making of peace is at least as costly as the making of war, at least as exigent, at least as disruptive, at least as liable to bring disgrace and prison and death in its wake.

"The only message I have to the world is: we are not allowed to kill innocent people," he told the court during his Plowshares Eight trial.

> We are not allowed to be complicit in murder. We are not allowed to be silent while preparations for mass murder proceed in our name, with our money, secretly. . . . It's terrible for me to live in a time where I have nothing to say to human beings except, 'Stop killing.' There are other beautiful things that I would love to be saying to people. There are other projects I could be very helpful at. And I can't do them. I cannot. Because everything is endangered. Everything is up for grabs. Ours is a kind of primitive situation, even though we would call ourselves sophisticated. Our plight is very primitive from a Christian point of view. We are back where we started. 'Thou shalt not kill'; we are not allowed to kill. Everything today comes down to that—everything.

I am very grateful to Wipf and Stock Publishers for republishing some of Dan's classic works in a series, books which influenced millions of people when they first appeared. I hope these books will be studied, passed around to friends and neighbors, and promoted far and wide. They still offer great hope, wisdom, and encouragement.

In the life and words of Daniel Berrigan we discover new faith in the God of peace and courage to pursue God's reign of peace. We see signs and guideposts for the path ahead, toward a new future of peace. And we find strength to take our own stand for justice and disarmament, to take another step forward on the road to peace and nonviolence. May these books inspire us to become, like Daniel Berrigan, peacemakers in a world of war.

—John Dear
Cerrillos, New Mexico
August 2007

CONTENTS

CONTENTS

Part One
A SPIRITUAL GEOGRAPHY

One

OPEN SESAME:
MY LIFE AND GOOD TIMES

My brother Philip and I were two of six brothers. We were depression babies, all of us. My father used to say that in the thirties he had lost everything but his shirt. If that was so, we must also recall with a certain wry humor that he only had one or two shirts to lose.

We lived most of our lives in a sixty-year-old house on the top of a hill, surrounded by ten not very fruitful acres. I remember vividly that we housed and fed a continuing number of homeless men during those dark years of loss. Even those neighbors who would not themselves feed or clothe or house the poor would always tell them that they could find something at our place.

Our schooling was mediocre at best. But it was augmented by constant reading. My mother deserves an eternal reward for the constant tonnage of books she carried home by streetcar from the city library.

Our life was frugal and untidy, with regular cleanups on my father's part to reassert his iron brand of authority. But it was always something like a roundup of colts. The fact is that he was not home a great deal of the time, and we generally ran free.

I entered the Society of Jesus in 1939. I was acquainted with no Jesuits, so it was a matter of an act of faith on both sides. Not a bad arrangement.

As with any young person of eighteen entering upon an entirely new form of life, the memories of my first years are particularly vivid. With regard to present convictions, I think they gave me a deep sense of the presence of God in the world, and most especially in human community. I must say too that I fell in love immediately and incurably with the Jesuit style, although prior to my entrance I had practically no knowledge of it first-hand. But it appealed to me immediately as a ground for my boundless idealism; and I found in the talents and youth and drive around me a constant spur to make my own life count.

When I entered upon my studies it became clear that I had a great deal of ground to catch up and win. Practically all of my classmates had graduated from Jesuit schools in the New York or Buffalo areas. They were invariably far ahead of me on almost every criteria that counted for achievement in our Bruderhauf.

I passed three miserable years at Woodstock College studying philosophy. It was simply not my dish. So I languished like an unhappy three-year freshman, trying with varying degrees of desperation and moodiness to find myself in a thicket of logic and metaphysics. I finished that period with enormous relief and almost entire lack of distinction.

I taught high school for three years, 1946–49, in St. Peter's Preparatory School, Jersey City, New Jersey. As I recall, I taught French, Latin, English, and what was fondly called, at that time, "religion." Everything I had believed or hoped about my-self, by way of being a contributory creature in the real world, began to come true. I struck out in every direction, like a belated flower child. And this at the hands of some three hundred rough and tough Jersey kids. It was indeed the first of many miracles.

With some misgivings, I undertook theological studies at West College, at Weston, Massachusetts, in the autumn of 1949. I was then twenty-eight years old, ten years away from my initial decision to enter the order; three years awaited me until ordina-tion, five years until the completion of the ordinary Jesuit regime of studies. So it was as a kind of ageless elephant that I lumbered into this other phase and began anew. There is nothing of distinction to report of those next years. The courses were in the main mediocre, with some exceptions in scriptural studies. I was finally (and from my point of view miraculously) ordained to the priesthood on June 19, 1952. Another year of theology and rustication in the same green acres. And a year later, in July of '53, I departed for a year of studies in France.

Although I did not realize it for the space of several months, my real mind was being implanted, the future was being furiously sown. It was a tumultuous and even catastrophic year for French society and the French Church. Pius XII was bearing down heavily upon the worker priests; he finally suppressed the movement entirely in February of 1954. The French were living through the dying spasms of Dienbienphu. The end of the Indo-Chinese colonial adventure was at hand, and the republic was stricken at the heart, to a degree it had not known since the crisis of occupation and Vichy. It was a year of national humiliation and turmoil.

Our house of studies near Lyon was as poor as any church mouse dwelling. But we had a sense of sharing in something extraordinarily painful in France at large. Many of my compatriots were survivors of German exploitation, and had worked in labor camps and factories under the occupier. Almost everything I experienced was being experienced for the first time. I felt in many cases as though I had landed upon a new planet, and was being asked to operate in an entirely new way, to rebuild my senses, my very soul. It was not merely a matter of fumbling about with a new language and slowly gaining confidence in it. The truth was that the language offered new ways into the world of other human beings—and that these others, penetrated and formed by a thousand-year history expressed in their lucid and vivid language, were also new beings, into whose community I was invited to enter. The invitation was austere but irresistible.

What I discovered in France for the first time in my long experience of Catholic community was so simple a thing as personal freedom. It was an invitation to become a human being by way of others, immersed as we all were during that year in the tradition of our scripture, as well as the experience and history of our Order.

In retrospect that year is bathed in a glow of idyllic personal light. The actuality was somewhat more gritty. It must be confessed that in February of 1954 I sojourned into West Germany and became party to our vast military complex there. I served for some two months as an auxiliary chaplain; thoughtlessly and with a naïve acceptance that had nothing to do, as I look back, with the cruel realities of that land and time. I preached and heard confessions and counseled innumerable soldiers—and never once brought up, or had brought up to me, the question of modern war, the question of why we were in Germany at all. I do remember writing home from Germany that the endless expenditures and installations, including the first nuclear installation in Western Europe, reminded me ominously of the advance of the Roman Empire. In order to come up with such a thought, I must have entertained at the time rather serious misgivings about the whole adventure. But I cannot claim an acuity of conscience that was only to come to me much later. The fact is that at the time I enjoyed those months; I thought the soldiers who crossed my path and with whom I dealt were unusual and delightful fellows. As undoubtedly they were.

More germane to what I can only call the retardation of my development was the influence upon me of the chaplains I was assisting. I remember that every one of them, without exception, was totally militarized. They wore their uniform not solely upon their frame, but upon their soul. It was a symbol of the state of their spirit. They were as military as their colleagues in the Officers' Clubs, and in church on Sunday. Indeed, it seemed to me even at the time that several of them made an especially severe push to project themselves as military men to the core—especially the head chaplain, who was a Jesuit of the New York area, fitted this mold to the very cap. He was a lieutenant colonel, a tireless worker, and had an astonishing influence over the young soldiers. He used to drive all night to a mountain retreat with groups of them to preach a retreat that many of them declared had brought their lives to rebirth. He would drive back with them through the night following the close of their spiritual exercise. Alas, he died later of overwork, and I have no doubt that the judgment upon him is merciful. But it seems to me also that he was a captive of the military system, that his life never once raised the questions that lie at heart of the gospel.

I returned to New York in the autumn of 1954 and began to teach at Brooklyn Preparatory School. For three years, I undertook work with teams of students among the Puerto Ricans of Brooklyn, and on the Lower East Side of Manhattan. We also instituted an honors system of studies in the school, which later won some distinction as the students went on to university work.

In the autumn of '57 I reported for teaching at Le Moyne College in Syracuse, New York. In a sense I felt that now my life was beginning on an entirely fresh and exciting basis. I was teaching college classes for the first time; the college was only eleven years old, and we were, in a rather innovating way, making go as we went. I was assigned to teach New Testament classes.

The following six years were an intense, even incandescent continuum—between the classroom on campus and the communities in rural Mexico, between my work in Syracuse and the work of my brother Philip in New Orleans. I cannot remember when I was more hardily tested or more blessedly renewed in spirit. For six long years I was riding the crest of a wave toward a shore that continually receded and expanded, showing now its reefs, now its populated and noisy centers, now the human faces upon its shore, inviting or threatening.

I think I had the reputation of being a very demanding teacher. I think too that my mind was still in a kind of mind set. I know I always resented being referred to as a teacher of "dogmatic" theology. But the fact was that I was still, in many aspects, quite dogmatic. And that is the one regret that I have when I ponder those years. For the rest, I continued to grow, still very much in my own nest, with all the possibilities both of befouling and of building it.

In 1957 I won the Lamont Prize for my first book of poetry. This was an enormous stimulus upon work that up to then had been wrought mainly in darkness. With the publication of my first book my mind exploded. The poems went into three printings, were a nominee for the National Book Award, and established me in the publishing world. Publishers would now take almost anything I chose to compile; the question of quality was largely in my own hands and my own sense of things.

Of interest with respect to the tumultuous years that were to follow is the fact that David Miller was one of my students. At least one thousand students passed through my classes in those six years. But it is not to be wondered at that I remember David quite vividly. The question of war had not yet occurred; Vietnam was still a remote and obscure event. David, however, was part of whatever social action was occurring off-campus, or being planned on-campus.

His was a poor family; as far as I can recall his parents were separated. The family lived in public housing, and David eked out his college career with state loans. My name has been associated with him in the years that followed, and I am indeed proud of whatever that may be construed to imply, even of guilt by association. The fact is that we never discussed war and peace; we often discussed civil rights and tried to do something about the horrendous ghetto conditions of downtown Syracuse. I can only reflect upon the mystery that has since become a little more apparent. That is to say, David's life was fertile soil upon which the good seed fell and flourished.

Toward the new year of 1962 I was granted a go-ahead with a project of living off-campus with fifteen students who would prepare themselves for Peace Corps type of work in rural areas of Mexico. We got the house off to a flying start, built a simple chapel in the basement, and settled into the chancy business of making ourselves into a community. It went well.

By the time I left Le Moyne for Europe in the summer of 1963, things were proceeding well, and the first team had already gone south.

I come now to the discussion of another watershed in my life. According to all plans, I was to lead a rather stereotyped year abroad in a Jesuit house, reportedly finishing a book and undertaking another. Those well-laid plans!

After some two weeks of searching for housing in Paris, I finally was able to find a student hostel and a job as chaplain.

By Christmas I had decided that Western Europe was no longer my cup of tea, and that if I was to get anything out of the year I had better launch southward and eastward. And so I did. At Christmastime I visited Czechoslovakia and Hungary for periods of about one week each. It was my baptism in Marxist society. I was particularly moved by the evidence that the churches in those countries, especially the Protestant communities, were finding ways of survival in most difficult circumstances. I returned to Paris by way of Rome, in order to report to the Vatican on what I had discovered in Eastern Europe. It amounted to a very strong recommendation on the part of the Protestant communities that the Vatican begin to take a more practical interest in the religious and social situation in Marxist Central Europe. I reported to Cardinal Bea's assistant, a man who later became a bishop. He gave me a sympathetic hearing. I was trying to interest the church officials in the idea that I should be appointed a Vatican observer at the Christian Peace Conference to be held in the summer of 1964. Alas for those great hopes.

However, I did get to Prague in June of '64, and proceeded with a group of American theologians into the Soviet Union, by invitation of the Orthodox and Baptist communities there. The impact of that trip is ineradicable upon my spirit. I was discovering for the first time, and at firsthand, the radically different social forms by which other decent men and women were living. I was discovering peaceable communities of faith, surviving and even thriving in most difficult and trying circumstances. I was seeing at firsthand the damage wrought to the human spirit in the West as a result of the Cold War.

At Prague, I met with Christians from both Marxist and Western societies, and gained some inkling of the role that the churches could play in the ongoing struggles for human peace and survival. Along with my American companions, I was also exposed to the full glare of world Christian opinion with regard to our part in the Vietnam war. From Japan to Cuba, Christians were assailing us, extremely embittered at the course that even then seemed to be written in our stars.

At the conclusion of that trip, I traveled to Africa, the second extended trip I had made during the year. This time it was western Africa, to Nigeria. (Toward Eastertime of the previous spring, I had gone along the coast of eastern Africa to the Republic of South Africa, at the invitation of an archbishop there.)

I returned to the United States in the autumn of 1964 convinced, as I now recall, of one simple thing. The war in Vietnam could only grow worse. The course we had set at the initiative of John Kennedy, and more remotely by Dulles's brinkmanship and by the nuclear fervor of Truman—all of this was about to turn in the direction of a war which we were in no mood to limit or to abandon. From one point of view, it struck me that we were about to repeat the already bankrupt experience of the French, with a new provocation and a new rhetoric. From another point of view, we were altogether masters of our own method. We had nothing like the colonial interests that France had had in Southeast Asia. But we were determined, justified as we were by the course and momentum of the war itself, to prove our manhood and to put to the test our formidable military machine. It is extraordinarily difficult, even years later, to attempt to unravel the tortuous symptoms and motivations that edged us even deeper into that remote morass. But the unraveling of that tangled and tightened skein is not to my purpose here.

I am attempting merely to record that, for me, the course of the future was made plain by everything I had experienced in Europe and throughout other continents. That is to say, I began after my return to the States in the autumn of 1964, as loudly as I could, to say "no" to the war. It is always, of course, an extremely difficult and risky business to try to relive things, from the point of view of one's life, once events have been lived through. But I am still near enough to those decisions, and still enduring their consequences, so I have a realistic hope that I can convey these experiences with reasonable accuracy. I remember being afflicted with a sense that my life was being truly launched—for the first time—upon mortal and moral seas that might indeed overwhelm me, as the tidal violence of world events churned them into an even greater fury. And even in those years, when we were speaking hypocritically of "military advisers to the Vietnamese," I had a sense that the war could not but get worse. I felt that we were even then launched upon a suicide course; we were spoiling for a fight; we were determined not to yield before a poor and despised people, whose "underdeveloped, non-white status" made them prime expendable targets. I felt (and I believe I shared this conviction with my brother Philip) that this war would be the making or breaking of both of us. There would be simply no turning back upon the initial serious moves we were making at that time.

I was even then signing statements of complicity, and opening myself to the kind of prosecution that Benjamin Spock and William Sloane Coffin were later to undergo.

Within a year's time, I had taken part in the forging of those methods of protest against the war which, from our present vantage point, we perhaps are justified in calling conventional. We fasted, marched, picketed, sat in, followed every step of escalation as well as we could with our halting methods and means; at least we were dogging the iron heel of Mars. We never succeeded, and we never quite gave up. That is the best that can be said for us. We must be content if it is to be our obituary.

Of course, the ground was shifting under my feet. My conception of history and of moral action was being altered, even as I strove to act. The old, tidy, well-arranged box of the universe was flying open, and the seven plagues were loosened upon the world. There would be no closing that box again. There could only be an attempt to follow the course of evil and the death with whatever trail mercy and compassion might blaze.

Nor could I convey the electric and terrifying quality of the times merely by saying that my relationship to my Church and my Order were being profoundly reordered. The fact is, two cents plain, that we were helping to create a new Church, and a new Order. American Catholics had never before, in the history of American wars, been found wanting. They were doubly patriotic because they were Catholic, and once had been commonly branded as somewhat less than American. The epitome of this older Martian spirit was of course the cardinal archbishop of New York, then alive and flourishing. It was entirely predictable that he and I, coming from backgrounds that were interesting in their common aspects, he exercising enormous authority in the same area in which I was saying "no" to the war, should come into conflict. The fact that the conflict would be scaled down to my size in no way put off the conflict. My "no" was being heard despite the sound of his immensely more powerful and permeating "yes." So it came to pass that only one year after my return to New York, I found myself faced with the most severe crisis of my life up to that time. It is almost impossible, even at this date, to unravel the many threads that were weaving my shroud. The suffocating descent of that shroud about my head and body came about, I am certain, as a result of my peace activities. Among these, and evidently a source of great friction, was the fact that I had helped found Clergy and Laymen Concerned about Vietnam during the previous summer.

Then there was the mysterious affair of the death of Roger La Porte. He was a boy whose face I remember remotely at the edges of the crowd of young people on the Lower East Side who were resisting the war. He had recently left a monastery upstate and was seeking to discover his own soul among the young Catholic workers. He had said to someone, as I recall, that he wished to get to know me better. But we had scarcely even spoken, apart from greeting one another on occasion. Then without warning, he immolated himself, in early November, before the United Nations buildings in New York early one morning. He lived for about three days. Within a week or two, the most atrocious rumors were linking his death to his friendship with me. It was not to be wondered that a time of growing national madness, was also infecting us, on our own scene.

In any case, about a week before Thanksgiving, I was ordered out of New York and within a week was aboard a jet for Mexico City, bound for indefinite exile.

I spent about five months in Latin America. I traveled throughout ten countries, observing and writing. The story of those months is told in a later book, *Consequences: Truth and . . .* In the meantime, opinion in my behalf in the Catholic community had become so unified and pressing, that my superiors were forced to recall me. An ad appeared in the New York *Times* challenging the Archdiocese of New York and the Jesuit community as to their reasons for my hasty exit. The protest was effective. I was able to return, held a large press conference to announce the publication of two new books, and say that beyond doubt I would continue with my peace work as usual.

Which I did. The war had worsened. My brother had been evicted from the seminary where he was teaching in Newburgh, New York. He had published his first book, which had been well received, we had marched in Selma, heard the President announce on television "We shall overcome." I had returned to the work of building a community of alternatives in New York and throughout the country. The éclat surrounding my exile had stimulated a number of invitations to address campus groups throughout the country, and I responded as well as I could. I was writing and being published, finding that a great deal of imprisoned space in my psyche had been released through the dark experience of the previous year. It was, all in all, a time of great anguish and great exhilaration.

In the summer of 1967, I went to Pueblo, Colorado, to teach in the Upward Bound program. I had been associated with poverty programs at the national level before this, but I wished to ground myself in immediate work with a small number of young people. Previously, I had journeyed throughout California and met with perhaps ten or twelve examples of diverse communities which the Office of Economic Opportunity was trying to help. If I bring in this aspect of my experience, it is only to underscore my growing disillusionment with national programs to "help the poor." Also my growing sense, expressed to Mr. Sargent Shriver on many occasions, that his program would get nowhere as long as the war was on. It seemed to me spiritually absurd and suicidal to be pretending to help the poor at home while we bombed the poor abroad. This seemed to me the deepest reason for the forewritten doom of the OEO.

In any case, uncertain as to what the next year would bring, I taught some fourteen young Mexican Americans from a poverty-stricken area of the town. My success was at best mixed. I gained additional fuel for my conviction that serious involvement in the poverty program was an inevitable source of alienation for the poor themselves, as well as being a money and land grab for the bureaucrats. Neither in Pueblo nor anywhere else in the country had I ever seen a poverty program whose leadership were part of the community of the poor. Once they began to draw a federal salary, the "leaders" inevitably were cut off from the best of their own community, and appeared, at least to the radicals and activists among them, as simply copouts. Thus for the dreams, liberal and unattainable, of the OEO.

I finally was invited by Cornell University in the autumn of 1967 (the first Catholic priest in the history of the university) to take a position in the United Religious Work. I left New York with trepidation and many second thoughts. It appeared to me a choice of the utmost seriousness, to decide to leave the peace community, which was in perennial need of all kinds. But I decided to come, because Cornell was a new scene to me, and because the university had changed so rapidly in the previous two years. I must say that I have never had a serious regret for the choice I then made.

But the war was going from horrendous to intolerable; it was devouring more and more of the energies of our lives.

My brother Philip was working in the inner city of Baltimore; a community man, he drew the community around him like a magnet. The facts of life were his daily bread. He saw in his prophetic bones that our support of the student resisters was a game the government would tolerate indefinitely. So in November 1967 he and three friends decided to take their peaceable war into the enemy camp. As is by now well known, they poured blood into draft files in Baltimore.

I was at the time very far from their understanding of things. But I was shaken into reflectiveness. I had gone to Hanoi, I had experienced American bombings and brought home prisoners of war. So when Philip approached me in early May with a new action into which I was urgently invited, my immediate reaction was one of bewildered sympathy and shaken readiness. I was faced with the evidence of intransigent courage on the part of those who were already in legal trouble up to their very necks. Imagine Philip and Tom Lewis, men already under threat of several years of imprisonment, calmly repeating the same action that had brought them into jeopardy!

Like a shipwreck or a man sucked into quicksand or a drowning man, to whom almost every resource of friendship and ingenuity is lacking, and yet who somehow emerges alive, I say simply that I was saved at the last moment.

In speaking analogically, I mean to speak no less rigorously. I was saved at the last moment. My brother and his friends were planning a new assault upon a new draft center. They visited me at Cornell toward the middle of May 1968. There, over a long evening of eating and discussion, they made their proposal to me. Would I join them? I was still wedded to the idea that in standing with the resisting students I was doing all that was possible, or indeed helpful. But after the others had left, Philip opened before me the facts of the case, which he had so often outlined in correspondence with me. That is to say—it must be evident by now that the government would allow men like myself to do what we were doing almost indefinitely; to sign statements, to picket, to support resisters in court. Even if they did pick us up, it was the government who were choosing the victim and the time and place of prosecution. The initiative was entirely in their hands. But in the plan under discussion, the situation was entirely reversed. A few men were declaring that the initiative of action and passion belonged to the peaceable and the resisting.

Toward dawn, I can remember seeing the light. I told Philip that I was with them. They should allow me some twenty-four hours to subject my decision to possible change of mood, but if they had not heard from me within that period, they could assume that I would be a member of the Catonsville group. And so, as the Book of Genesis says laconically, it was done.

We nine invaded the draft office, took out hundreds of 1-A files, and burned them with homemade napalm in a macadam parking lot nearby. I remember so well the heat and fury of that afternoon, and the sense of almost crushing relief with which we faced one another after it was done.

I remember also, when we had been apprehended and put in temporary custody, the expressions on the faces of the F.B.I. men as they entered and saw us clerics under arrest, the familiar face of Philip, previously apprehended in a like cause. How their jaws dropped! One of them turned in disgust to a companion and exclaimed, "I'm going to change my religion." Which was, I would think, entirely to our point; we had invited men to a change of heart, so that in the case of this officer, to have changed from a conventional Catholic to a Christian, might portend the first success of our efforts.

We spent eight days in Baltimore County jail in Towson, Maryland. We fasted and prayed and rejoiced—and waited.

I remember with special gratitude the warden, Stephen Foster. He was consistently good to us, puzzled as he was by our action, and of a curious integrity, which drove him to question and discuss with us why we had placed our lives in the breach.

I remember also that on the final day we decided to break our fast with a Eucharist. Someone had brought us in a loaf of freshly baked bread. We asked the warden if we might have a bottle of wine. He acceded on condition that he himself might be present for our Eucharist. Of course he might. Whereupon, around that board table, began one of the simplest and most moving of communal actions. "Do this in memory of me." Which is to say; "In remembering me, re-member yourselves. Put your lives and your souls together again."

The unpredictable savagery of a federal marshal is also vivid in my mind. One day, as we were being taken handcuffed from the jail for a court appearance, a young nun who was a dear friend reached out her hand to mine in solidarity as we issued from the jail. One of the marshals came forward in a swift, reptilian move. He crashed down between our hands with a karate blow. "Don't touch!" It was the epitome of the system; he had said it all.

Don't touch—make war. Don't touch—be abstract, about God and death and life and love. Don't touch—make war at a distance. Don't touch your enemy, except to destroy him. Don't touch, because in the touch of hand to hand is Michelangelo's electric moment of creation. Don't touch, because law and order have so decreed, limiting the touch of man to man, to the touch of nightsticks upon flesh. . . .

It must be evident by now, that the most powerful and immediate influence upon my life has been that of my brother Philip. Indeed, his incarceration for some seven months after Catonsville, placed my own spirit in bondage. It was many weeks before I could realize that being free was also a way of allowing a larger freedom for him. But I must say also that upon this single relationship has been built every other one in which my life rejoices.

Another weight upon the decision to go to Catonsville was my voyage to Hanoi in February of 1968. I went with Howard Zinn of Boston University, to repatriate the first American fliers freed by the North Vietnamese. I will not linger over particulars here; they are told in some detail in my book, *Night Flight to Hanoi*.

I have referred elsewhere in the course of our federal trial, to a third event that shook my existence in those months. It was the self-immolation of a sixteen-year-old boy in front of the Syracuse Cathedral in the spring of 1968. I visited him as he lay dying in St. Joseph's Hospital. And I smelled, for the first time, and yet again not for the first time, the odor of burning flesh, evidence of which I had seen so often in North Vietnam. The boy died, but not before he had brought something to birth in me. Perhaps it is that day, that youthful dying face, whose wordless intimations I am still undergoing and undoubtedly shall for years to come.

I am, in this autumn of 1969, under federal sentence of three years, for destruction of draft files in May of 1968. So my life enters upon its middle course. These many beautiful years cannot be lived again. But they are compounded in my own flesh and spirit, and I take them, in true measure, with me toward whatever lies ahead.

I have by now had published thirteen books on a variety of subjects, have written numerous articles and poems and plays, and have enjoyed all the fruits that America offers those fortunate enough to make it within her system. If I mourn for the death of that system, it is as one who has enjoyed its cup to the depths. If that same vintage has now turned bitter as gall in my mouth, it is because I have seen the society that might have been great, according to its own rhetoric, turn murderously against those throughout the world to whom it had once offered the fairest of hopes. I could no longer drink the fruit of those grapes that had turned to wrath against the majority of men; that murderous vessels of death even now tipping upon victims in North Vietnam, ready elsewhere to deal the same death to other men whose hopes were too revolutionary or too untimely to be borne with.

If then I must go to prison (and go I undoubtedly must),

I shall go neither in a spirit of alienation, of bitterness, nor of despair. But simply in the hope that has sustained me in better and worse days up to now. May this offering open other alternatives to official and sanctioned murder, as a method of social change. May men of power come to a change of heart, confronting the evidence and quality of the lives we offer on behalf of our brothers.

Two

THE BEST OF TIMES,
THE WORST OF TIMES

I had just returned from answering one of my frequent summonses on law and order at Jesuit headquarters. As usual, things
were not good. I went to a Jesuit friend and told him so, in
mournful numbers. He answered laconically: "Do you want to
know why you're in trouble so frequently?" I swallowed hard
and averred I did not. He said, "It's because you and some
others show us what Jesuits can be. And that's why we can't
stand you."

Now when things get really bad (like every day), I run to
Mother Hubbard's cupboard to take out that old bone. It never
fails me, a cold comfort indeed.

I gnaw a question, like a dog a bone. Can it be that we
have come to an impasse where we can't really bear with our
own brothers, can't hear them out, respect what they do? Have
they so outgrown us, or have we so ingrown on one another, on
somnolent communities, on gothic campuses, on outer space mis-
sions and rendezvous, on moral weightlessness; on absence, absence—absence from other lives, from different scenes, different
passions, different visions of life; to the point where *we* and *they*
are brute facts of armed neutrality, and *I* and *thou* are forbidden
topics?

It is one of the hardest, most persistent questions of my life.
I come no nearer, day after day, to the resolution of a knot
that seems dipped in blood and tightened like a noose. Is one's

community reformable? And can one survive in it, as a human being whose vocation, like human respiration, moves both in and out?

The question is not, of course, solely a Jesuit question. But its first analogate is undoubtedly the Jesuits. The biggest, most influential and inventive of the Orders ought to be able to show us something—that we can make it, and that if we make it, others can. Or, as the dark side of the same question, if the Jesuits can't make it, can any others?

For instance, the Christian Brothers. With us in jail in Baltimore County after the burning of the draft files was Brother David Darst. He is my candidate for all-weather Christian. He is also the youngest of our nine, a *summa cum laude* graduate of a Minnesota college. All the good ingredients Christ puts in a man to make him his man are David's: guts, heart, brains, salt of humor. In previous months, he had handed in four successive draft cards—no incense to Mars, not even a pinch. He had survived the blandishments and threats of his local board, those old men who send the young off to die. David left the Towson jail after our week there, for his inner city school in St. Louis. Within some days he was plucked from his classroom by federal marshals and jailed once more, this time for refusing induction.

"Lord," asked Abraham in despair and hope, "for the sake of one just man will you save the city?"

David promptly began another fast in his new quarters, for some four days, while his Order let him sit. The young resisters of St. Louis finally scraped his bail together to get him out. The story has a certain piquancy, for the bursar of the St. Louis province of David's Order last year made a million dollars for Christ on the stock market. In such ways do Pauline charisms work today, their wonders to perform.

Later, my own provincial announced that the Jesuits would neither pay my bail nor censure me for my part in the draft board imbroglio. I was an admirable man, my superior averred to a friend, but I kept dragging the Society into these things. David's provincial had roughly the same to say of him, with an ominous nuance in the preposition: He kept dragging *down* his Order.

Any connection between such sentiments and the New Testament awaits a more thorough exegesis than I am at present capable of.

In the meantime, the cardinal of Baltimore stripped my brother of his priestly faculties. Philip could neither preach, hear confessions, nor offer Mass in public, even for his fellow prisoners— his only possible congregation, since he had been refused bail for some seven months, even after appeal to the Supreme Court. The warden of Towson jail, a man uninstructed in chancery niceties, mourned publicly for a lost chance. Since Philip had been sentenced, the prisoners had attended Mass in greater numbers than ever before; there seemed to be some connection, too subtle for those in power to grasp, quite lucid to the imprisoned, between the Eucharist and a priest who was a fellow prisoner. In protest, the jailed men refused to attend the Mass of an assigned outsider.

In sum, in a time of crisis, the Church had waited on the culture. When the war-making society had completed its case against a nonviolent, protesting priest, the Church moved against him too, sacred overkill added to secular. Indeed, Christ made common cause with Caesar; religion preached a new crusade, a dubious and savage war. The Church all but disappeared into the legions.

But not quite disappeared. For in this instance, as the President of the United States understands so well, the Church is a powerful ally. If to the enormous, pervasive seduction of wartime rhetoric, war economy, war appeals to common cause—if to these the sanction of God's will be added, then war has indeed become total; its claim on man's soul is beyond rational debate. As for those who protest, they live and die "outside the walls"; they are men without a country and a church. They can flee the nation or languish in jail; the curse of the inquisitor will penetrate the jails to strike them there. They will be removed from the grand design of salvation, the ennobling common patrimony of the faithful.

An old, old story—Joan of Arc; Thomas More; "Jäggerstätter; the protesting Jesuits in Hitler's Germany. No angel of the Lord sprung them; such Christians died, in almost every instance, unconsoled and unsupported by their communities. Cold comfort; death, then rehabilitation.

In a sense, though, all this is beside my point. Rather than pursue the theme, I recall once more the question that makes my entire life an exodus, a darkness. Is one's community reformable? Who indeed will rehabilitate the authority that puts on, not the mind of Christ, but the mindless method of Caesar?

A Jesuit said to me recently (and his words were a source of immense anguish): "If it is impossible to do the things you do, and win the support of the Society, then indeed superiors are hastening the end of the Order. For what man who values his humanity would enter an Order that forbids him to do what good men are impelled to do?"

One weekend, the Catonsville defendants currently at large on bond met in the New York area to plan the issues of their defense, and to consult with friends on matters of support. The sessions went on all day Saturday, and far into the night. On Sunday we did something of more import and better sense; we went on a picnic. In a green and pleasant place, far from the dolorous past weeks and the testing ahead, we played badminton, swam, and fooled with the children. Finally, as evening came on, we gathered in a circle, about a cup of wine and some dark bread. First some readings; Phil's letter from jail, an interview with Castro, Bonpane on Camilo Torres, a sermon of Vincent Harding, a poem of Neruda. Then the words of Christ; we passed the bread and cup.

You will grant us this much, in a time of the breaking of hearts—the breaking of bread.

It was my father's eighty-ninth birthday. At the time it was possible that he and my mother might not see Philip again.

They are feeble, and live at some distance from his jail, and he was just beginning his six-year sentence.

Yet, I must confess, I have no tears to shed for such actualities. Indeed, I almost said "no tears to waste." The difference is a considerable one. I have tears to shed for the victims of war, for the napalmed children, for the innocents of Saigon under rocket terror, for the Viet Cong decapitated by smiling GIs, for the plastic sacks piled like cord wood at Khesan, for the burning, broken land, the proud and gentle culture blasted to rubble.

But no tears for my family. My mother and father are not victims of anything, including life. They are lifegivers; they gave us life, and then gave us with a certain tender rigor to the service of life itself. So their old age exhibits a kind of moral edge, an unshakable human beauty. Things must be so, they aver; and the necessity is both Grecian and Christian; so must all justice be accomplished. The twilight of the gods, which defines our nation, is high noon for man; say "Alleluia."

Our parents were never corrupted by the cultural status-seeking that often demeans the priest and his family today. Some thirty years ago, my mother said to me with regard to a certain parish priest: "If you are going to be like him, don't go into it at all." When Phil and I refused to escalate ambition, they rejoiced. When we sought to go on a freedom ride, my father wanted to go along, and my mother said mildly: "At least let us know where you are from time to time." They were in every crucial instance pious, secular, and right. After such a home, and in spite of all official judgments of the powers, we could not go entirely wrong. Or so we thought, and think.

Today, in *manus tuas*. Our lives are in His hands. We are wrestling with the encompassing, inhabiting devils that would claim the Church, but for Christ, as their evil own: fear, pusillanimity, violence, concupiscence, pride of life. We stand on the brink of the unknown; which is to say; things are normal, and good, and permissive of joy.

At his instruction, Philip's friends disposed of his few possessions: books, baggage, clothing, all. One friend said with a kind of despair: "He told us to give his clothing to the poor, but the poor couldn't get much use out of what he owned." Indeed, I knew he had bought nothing new to wear for several years. In court, he appeared in a picturesque suit of uncertain vintage, out at the elbows. Good sense; the prison system would see to his wants in the years ahead.

Someone said to me recently, after a discussion on our predicament: "Don't worry, we'll do something for you." His air was avuncular, and I was stung. By pride, perhaps; but I said with what gentleness I could summon: "Good; we've already done something for you."

Something for you. Something for the Church, something for the Josephites, something for the Christian Brothers, for the Jesuits, something for Maryknoll. Something for society, something for the Vietnamese, for the Africans, for the Latins, for the poor. Something for history. We have declared ourselves indigent before the courts. Whatever our friends can do for us, in legal proceedings that are bound to be expensive and drawn out—but that is their decision. The only present certainty seems to be that our Orders will do nothing; or next to nothing; they have foreclosed our credit, our claim on their compassion by whatever vow or ordination.

It may be thought that other friends will assemble about us. I think, as I write, of another man who came to the truth of things; late, but not too late for the winning of mercy; and who declared of the dead man Jesus: "This was surely a just and a good man."

May our conduct win to our persons a like tribute from those we love.

Three

TRIAL BY FIRE

The issues of our trial in Baltimore were not encompassed by the fate of the nine of us who stood accused . . . nor by the charges set against us. Legally, that was the business of the court. But the real issues centered around decency, justice, and community, not around charges rendered by the prosecution and decisions handed down by the jury.

These issues are neither new nor peculiar to the handful of us who faced sentencing in Federal Court in Baltimore on November 8, 1968. Rather, they are issues that younger people have brooded about with far greater risk and for a much longer time than we nine who entered upon them. And they are serious issues, indeed.

The present impasse of the traditional structures of society makes these issues crucial to whatever human future, whatever human hope we can claim. They are deeply embedded in American society itself and in the continuing experience of revolution. Expressed as they were in a rather dramatic way at the trial, they possibly form paradigms upon which we might judge where we are and where we are going. It is on this concrete basis I wish to lay stress.

The events leading up to the trial, as well as the trial itself, suggest a number of questions about American attitudes toward war and toward the law. Out of Catonsville—and our federal trial—emerge certain unanswered questions; how our posture toward Vietnam relates to a historic concept of war, how this concept both conditions and is conditioned by our perception of suffering and of death.

More; inherent in the courtroom proceedings are several possible paradigms about the role of the judicial system in American life. How do attitudes toward human justice and the letter of the law, as exemplified in this trial, reveal the general relationship of law and order to a healthy society? Does the failure of the law to deal with key questions of human life today, in this society, indicate what we can expect from other institutions, as they come to grips with parallel questions?

At the outset, we nine saw our action in a common light, both from the viewpoint of a community of faith and our views of the needs of society and of international life. We hoped our experiences would urge others to discover alternatives to the imposition of death, to the socializing of death, to the technologizing of death. We saw our action as a social method of achieving a future for man.

Many of us—myself from European, African, and Latin-American experiences—were sick unto death of death itself as a definition of the American way. We wanted to say, quite simply and clearly, at Catonsville, in the court, and in the prison that undoubtedly will follow, that something radically different is still possible, that we ourselves wished to offer a possibility of achieving that difference.

Also, from a background of many cultural and religious experiences (ranging from Guatemala to North Vietnam to Africa to Eastern Europe to the Soviet Union to the American ghettos), we were trying to converge in a single judgment about our society and its conduct in the world.—We wished to question our way of dealing with the living, and, by implication, with the unborn.

This intent arose at a time when Secretary of State Dean Rusk was emphasizing that Vietnam is an "exemplary war among developing peoples"—a war "from which light upon many other wars" may come. His phrase contains, it seems to me, two ominous predictions for us, one implied and the other spelled out by the eminent statesman in an article in *The Atlantic Monthly*.

The first implication is clear. Vietnam is a warning—a warning of the pace and direction, as well as the social and political structures, allowable in the developing world. It stands as an indication of the extent to which American determination, by every device of foreign policy, economic investment, and military finesse, will permit change among people desperately in need of rapid and radical socialization. Vietnam is a warning issued to the third world that those nations may not hasten or change their pace or direction unless the change is compatible with our vision of human history and human development.

Out of this "exemplary" nature of the war, there follows the practical tactics that Rusk dwelled upon. It is allowable, in a controlled war situation, such as Vietnam, to experiment with new weaponry. It is allowed to improve and discharge such weaponry upon civilian populations as a way of winning the war.

This being so, as three of the Catonsville defendants witnessed from the Latin-American scene, it is entirely possible that after this war is settled, a like war will break out elsewhere. As Dean Rusk has promised us, the American people may expect fifty years of "Vietnams" after this one.

In the discussions that went on for months in preparation for our trial, we concluded that if the principle of Rusk were accepted and his implicit methodology allowed to follow, we ourselves were obligated, by every canon known to civilized and Christian people, to interpose ourselves and our security. At such a time, we felt we must enter not only into conditions of risk with the young, but also into situations of suffering, separation, disgrace, and possibly even death. All this is the daily portion of soldiers here and general populations elsewhere if war is to flourish. The requirements have also grown more severe for peacemakers. So, from two points of view, we wanted to find a new kind of spiritual geography out of which to operate.

Modern war is total in principle and totalizing in effect. Throughout our history of wars, beginning with our own revolution, a preliminary requirement for a generation's being truly "American" was the demand that young people enter situations where death is the proximate risk.

And in the case of modern war, the word "total" had taken on even more ominous overtones. A third world war is no longer necessary, in order for war to be qualitatively total. Modern war in the nature of things totalizes its claim upon the person. Its rhetoric releases an atmosphere, a pollution; to breathe it is to die. And this totalizing effect must be created by analogy— in areas of growth, purity, clarity, and modesty—on the peace scene.

We realized, before we entered into social jeopardy, that there would be no opportunity for an open plea before the court. So we entered on the trial with different ambitions, a different vocabulary, and even, I dare to say, different spiritual resources. In principle, the courts, up to the U. S. Supreme Court itself, are unwilling, especially in wartime, to consider seriously the moral and legal questions of war itself. So we felt that civilized men must seek to use the courtroom in order to achieve some public audibility about who we were and what we were about. The issues raised by the war—issues of the constitutionality and morality of the war, of free speech and freedom of protest— might thereby be separated from our personal or corporate fates. We were obliged in fact to attain some kind of personal liberation before acting at all, a certain spiritual detachment from the fact of prison. So, in a sense, the scenario of the trial was written before the action itself occurred.

At the outset, we decided that the trial should be extremely brief . . . as brief as we could make it. We would have been satisfied and happy with a single day in court. We were trying to wave aside as irrelevant—as a kind of fatty excrescence upon the bone and musculature of our cause—all those legal devices by which one equivocates about what he actually has done or said.

So, on the first day, we abstained from the formalities of selection of jury, allowing the first twelve (fifteen including alternates), to be chosen among those who came forward. Whatever questioning of prospective jurors occurred was in the hands of the prosecution and the judge. As early as possible, we sought to dramatize in a hopeful way our indifference to our own fate.

From the outset, we sought to identify ourselves with those in the streets and the ghettos, with those who face the draft, prison, war or exile, and, indeed, with all the poor and powerless, with those at the outer end of our "merciful" activity in economics, politics, militarism, and diplomacy throughout the world. We tried to achieve clarity about our own faith, to manifest a visible unity between the events in the courtroom and those who had gathered by the thousands in the city to support us, and, by implication, between ourselves and the larger world of victims created by the war.

Against the long haul of human existence, we took a minute step in the direction of humanization. We told our stories as simply and directly as we could. We related how, from many different points of the compass, from different ages, different traditions, we had converged upon one judgment. If the war were total, the peace also must be total in its claim upon the person. No longer could we place upon a certain group the burden of our original sin—the oldest sin of history, constantly reinvigorated, restated as original for each generation by the forging of a new language of hatred, division, and death.

Out of this came, I think, on the last day of the trial, a rather extraordinary exchange between defendants and judge. It was something that had never occurred before, not merely in the political trials of this war, but within anyone's memory in that courtroom. After the jury had retired with his charge, the judge invited us to speak in open court about our impression of the trial, the issues, and the reception we had received. For some ninety minutes, we engaged in a very heated, intense, and, at times, profound exchange with this old man, shaken by the rigorous days he had undergone in a case of great complexity, and fought with passion on both sides.

The verdict was delivered within the hour. It was entirely predictable: All defendants were found guilty on all counts. The trial nonetheless stands in a sense apart from its immediate outcome; it perhaps may serve as a symbolic moment, on behalf of a people who are increasingly unsure of their capacity for change. The judge's declaration that "the issues affected him profoundly as a man but could not be raised before him in his legal robes," stands as an example of the relationship of the legal structure to the health of society. And this, it seems to me, is another way of stating the only question worth raising in times of social crisis: Who are we as a people?

One thinks of our history: from the American Revolution through the nineteenth century and the bitter division of the War Between the States, the abolitionists, the shining case and and writings of Thoreau, the infinitely vexing question of individuals' entrance or non-entrance into World War II, to the present war. A society discovers itself mercilessly in the mirror of its crisis. There is no point in searching for identity in times of normalcy: We cannot really see ourselves in that clouded mirror of unexamined affluence and selfishness we commonly call peace.

No, we need to clear the mirror. We need to discover, in the encounter of life and death, what our attitudes toward one another are, toward the continuing adventure of men; whether we are acceding to the end of that venture. So in the present when the stench of the dying—the innocent, the children, the soldiers—is rising in our nostrils, it is particularly important, in this least auspicious moment, when ordinary men have the least inclination, time, and depth available for reflection, that we raise the questions central to man: What values govern us? What are our resources? How much dissidence can we bear as a sign of health? How many threats to property can we endure as a price of human amelioration? Can we distinguish the weight of human life from the weight of paper? In times of great stress, are we capable of judging the difference between property and human beings? Indeed, are we capable of admitting that threats to the law may be contributions to human life?

At one point in our exchange, the judge said, "Of course, you're good men. Of course, I honor you. Of course, the evidence of this day has been moving to all of us in the court. But these are not the questions."

I suggest that these are exactly the questions. Whatever the law may declare, we cannot separate questions of life and death from questions of the law itself. Whatever unexamined traditional concepts of law may declare, we cannot transform law courts into city morgues in which questions of passion, soul, and conscience are excluded in principle, and the bodies on the table undergo nothing more than an autopsy.

The question raised in the Baltimore court will continue to haunt us; it was not uncovered there; it is daily held up to contempt in the continuation of the war. Nonetheless, the ghost is not easily laid; the questions continue. How much reality can we bear? How much human variety, how many voices, how much of life's reality pressing against the windows and walls of the court from the larger world of despair and alienation outside—how much of that can we endure?

The trial itself, to borrow Dean Rusk's phrase, was exemplary. By such action as ours, by such debates and punishments, the law itself is being subjected to the scrutiny of revolutionary times. The law is being judged, and the judgment is a harsh one. The law is less and less useful for the living, less and less the servant of men, less and less expressive of that social passion which in the early days of Greek and Roman jurisprudence brought the law into corporate being and set it into the bloodline of man as a spiritual resource, independent of its own rhetoric, its own salvation, its own privilege and power—the instrument and servant of man.

In every generation, the law must renew itself in the guts of the living. Along with the Church, medicine, education, and all the means by which man declares himself man, the law must be remade in the imagination of those who purvey the law, those who violate the law, and those who suffer under the law, in order that the law itself become what it says it is: *corpus humanum*—a human body.

Whatever the trial may have achieved for other people, I think for us the experience was a great one—a passionate creation in a human furnace. We never indulged in the romantic hope that others would come to agree with us. Such a hope, it seemed to me, would have indicated a closure of mind upon our own method as a sole way. God knows, as many methods as good men may discover are required if we are to break the present impasse.

No, our hope was that other men would grow more thoughtful, that they would discover, in patient revolution, all the possibilities inherent in the university campus, the church, the inner city, in work with the poor, in work with white racists—discover, in fact, better methods than ours of saying roughly the same things.

When I was in Hanoi, one word recurred frequently and unexpectedly. That word was patience. "After all," the Vietnamese said in many ways and on many occasions, "revolution is a very long haul." The achievement of a decent society for them had been the work of a thousand years; it was by no means finished. Medieval occupation of their country by Chinese, later by the Japanese, French, and then today's occupation and division. The work is long and still incomplete after a millennium.

The reflection was meant as a courteous correction of our own sense of time, whose national history is but a day in comparison with theirs. It was a correction to our impatience and short-circuiting in favor of violence as a method of change. A correction of our spasm of impatience that the decent community, the just society be achieved today or tomorrow. No, they said, revolution is a patient venture.

I have thought frequently since then that we, in a rigorous and contemplative way, must continue to juxtapose those two great notions of patience and revolution. The example of a poor and dauntless people suggests not only that revolution is a patient project, but that patience itself is a revolutionary virtue.

Four

CONSCIENCE, THE LAW, AND CIVIL DISOBEDIENCE

Let us grant from the beginning the serious nature of this subject. Indeed, it is so serious that on its behalf many good men are driven against a wall—to death by violence, to prison in resistance to violence. Their blood and tears forbid us the luxury of an abstract debate.

May I begin with a postulate that may be uncomfortable, but which cannot in truth be avoided. The postulate is a place: Cornell Law School. The school is Anglo-Saxon, white, Western. It is rich by anyone's standards: in libraries, in professional savvy, in tradition, in public resources. It carries the weight of Gothic walls, and a special coloration in all seasons; as such, it is a member of a league named "Ivy." It has joined hands with certain other white, rich, Anglo-Saxon, Western, post-Christian, post-Gothic structures of law schools. They, all of them, house lawyers, students, books, and by implication a large measure of our future, if any. I pay this excellent arrangement my tribute, even though mine can be, ironically, only the tribute of a felon.

Such, in crude brief, is the geography.

I also have a scene. I have not come out of Jove's forehead, nor out of a stork's chimney. Indeed, if one can believe it, I come out of a tradition stern in point of law, and insistent in force of obedience. There are those who may have heard of us—the Society of Jesus. We have a name here and there.

Now, it may be convenient for the purposes of civil law, or

even of the Catholic Church, to consider me a freak, the kind
of biological sport who turns up now and then to confound even
the most artful selective process. Such may be the fact. Or, something else may also be of point. It may possibly be that the
legal tradition and mine are converging on a point of truth; that
we, both of us, are trying to make that point—equally perplexed,
perhaps even in jeopardy before a truth of which neither of us
is the keeper.

The question is one of tradition, my tradition and that of the
legal profession. I believe a man's possibility is in large part meas-
ured by the tradition he comes out of. I have said it repeatedly
on the Cornell campus; I have said it before the SDS, before the
religious communities, before the fraternities, before my own soul;
like it or not, we are what we have been. A man can claim to
be going somewhere only if he has come from somewhere. Alienation in any absolute sense can only be a source of dislocation
and irresponsibility.

To go somewhere, a man must come from somewhere. For
myself, if my claim to Christian tradition is valid, it is so only
because I am trying to embody that conception of citizenship and
faith that runs from Jesus to Paul to Galileo to Newman to
Teilhard to Pope John to myself. In the same way, if one claims
the Western legal tradition, it is because one embodies a spirit
that runs from the Magna Carta through English common law
on to Holmes and Frankfurter to oneself.

It perhaps goes without saying also that if one claims to be the
inheritor of his tradition, he is required to cast off the enticements
and lies that corrupt the tradition. For the reverse of our proposi-
tion is also true: A man can claim to have come from somewhere
only if he is going somewhere. Thus I must cast off the fury
and incoherence of the Inquisition, and lawyers presumably are
ridding themselves of the attitudes we inherit from slave laws. I
am trying to outgrow an inhuman priesthood—its mystification,
and its neglect of living men. And men of the law, I would think,
are casting off the enticements of big money, big names, ignorance
of the social currents and passions of the day, neglect of those

who run with man—the draft resisters, the black power students, those who are working their way through perplexity and inhumanity, to a possibly decent society.

All of this may of course be no more than empty rhetoric, in the light of our actual desires and motives. For it takes enormous courage and discipline and patience to be a man of tradition, in the sense we speak of, in whatever sphere of life. One of the difficulties is that every discipline, every aspect of man's public life tends today, of its own unchecked momentum, to claim man totally for itself. Lawyers like to believe that man is the sum of his laws; sociologists, that man is the sum of societal phenomena; philosophers, that man is defined by his wisdom or logic; believers, that man is his religion; nationalists, that man owes his life and well-being to the state; generals, that man must march against other men, to someone's tune. But I dare to suggest, reporting on the fact of life, that in order to be a man, it is sometimes necessary to escape from these definitions; to free the ghetto, to disobey the law, to disavow the race, to surpass the religion. In order to be a student it is necessary to disrupt Columbia. In order to be a citizen it is necessary to march in the streets of Chicago. In order to abide by law, it is necessary to confront the law. Such at least are the possibilities that men feel impelled to explore. Men disobey, disrupt, break laws. Are they thereby criminals in fact? Or is something deeper and more mysterious at work? Can lawbreaking in certain cases be a function of conscience?

The thesis thus follows on the facts of the times, which is not, of course, a way of denying that the argument remains arguable. It must, in order to vindicate itself, confront both the fact of the reluctant courts and of the passionate lawbreakers, the fact of black anger and of white intransigence, the fact of stalemated structures and of the unkillable, rising tide of man's hope.

Today, powerful forces of love and hatred are experimenting with the future of our society. No one can rationally suggest that a stalemate or compromise will be any sort of viable outcome. Indeed, no. Everything in history suggests that so neat a solution is self-defeating. It is untrue to events, to the pace of things, to the evidence before us. Indeed, revolution is the heart of that evidence: radical social change is the order of the day and the dream or nightmare of the night.

That was the order of my generation, too, and its nightmare. We came out of a kind of northern Appalachian poverty. In the thirties our family was a rural one, a part of the pandemic poverty of the great depression years. And we barely made it. We learned firsthand the near catastrophe of the "crash," the harsh, slow recovery of the Roosevelt years, the first moves toward social reform. We were the hands into which the New Deal was dealt. Public relief programs, the Civilian Conservation Corps, the Industrial Reconstruction Act; we ate our alphabet soup and were grateful for it, however thin it was drawn.

During those same years, while federal institutions were shaken to their foundations, another fact of life surrounded my family. We were members of a church whose main word, whether we or others liked it or not, was revolutionary. The revolution only really began to march much later. No matter, the bomb was buried; it needed only to be detonated. Meantime, we had to undergo the preliminaries of any revolution; which is to say, the possession of the field by reactionaries. The church revolution today is in debt to its most determined resisters, ironically enough. Francis Cardinal Spellman and Senator Joseph McCarthy were the precursors; they flourished, all but unchallenged, during the fifties. (During the same years, for those who could really look around, there were men like Maritain, Murray, and Pope John on the scene, pointing to something radical and new.) And then the sixties arrived, and the Vietnam war fueled itself into a fury. The Catholics joined communities of protest across the nation, a fire wall against that monstrous fire. The Boston Two, the Baltimore Four, the Catonsville Nine, the Milwaukee Fourteen, the Washington Nine, the New York Eight, the protests by Catholics, mainly priests, in Chicago, Newark, Brooklyn, Cleveland. Revolution? The score (let me be arrogant for a moment) is not a total loss.

But what of the revolution in law? The news is not good. I

suggest that the facts are nothing short of lamentable. Today the law, and the mentality of those who make and enforce and teach and study the law, is changing too slowly; the headlong facts of social change are edging them offstage.

But there is more bad news to be told; the law, as presently revered and taught and enforced, is becoming an enticement to lawlessness. Lawyers and laws and courts and penal systems are nearly immobile before a shaken society, which is making civil disobedience a civil (I dare to say a religious) duty. The law is aligning itself more and more with forms of power whose existence is placed more and more in question. Lawyers, law students, and law professors have not raised their voices with any audibility against a monstrous, illegal war.

So if they would obey the law, men are being forced, in the present crucial instance, either to disobey God or to disobey the law of humanity. Indeed, obedience to American law, as purveyed and parlayed by many lawyers, as enforced in many courts, as punished in many jails, exacts, in many crucial instances, the violation of the rudimentary common sense requirements of a civilized conscience.

The law allows, on the other hand, a weird and possibly ruinous kind of selectivity in enforcement. The criminal activity of many men in power goes unscrutinized, while those whose despair or alienation drives them into the streets are prosecuted with all possible rigor. Differing criteria? Double standards? Of course—whether in respect of promptness or of rigor, when the law is applied, say, to a policeman, an Afro-American, a corporation executive, a clergyman, a dissident student.

Some are co-opted in principle. Some are protected in principle. And the result is predictable. A man is driven to break the law as a strict requirement of being a man at all. The law turns its screws on the limbs of decent men. A few resolve on heroism, most settle for complicity, simply because they are not heroic. The legal system suppresses human decency as a societal resource, because good men are not able to be heroic men. They are forced into objective evil, into evil obedience, because the law that claims them is intent on—what? Survival? Prestige? Big money? The pursuit of power?

I should like to sharpen the issue. The law profession, I submit, is one among several professions that, in the larger world of men, are simply acting against man. The leading American law schools are producing large numbers of lawyers every year whose professional life is a hideout from social change and human issues. Such schools produce judges who prosecute men like my brother and myself, instead of prosecuting the men who are prosecuting a genocidal war. They produce lawyers who peddle the American line at the United Nations, at embassies throughout the world, in government programs that mask or openly purvey retrograde nationalistic aims, compounded of militarism, nationalism, limited but no less looting wars. And if the present is any measure of the future, such schools strengthen a corporate system bent in the direction of more and more American economic hegemony abroad, more and more firmly imbedded poverty and racism at home.

The law profession, in fact, is connecting with fewer needs, fewer issues, and fewer men. Need we linger over the dolorous fact that the legal profession has just produced a new President of the United States? Charity, or depression of spirit, forbids further comment.

Now the really dolorous fact is not that Mr. Nixon is an anomaly; in the legal profession, as lawyers advance toward power, Mr. Nixon is, in fact, typical. He is, in fact, pure American, vintage 1970. Within an arrangement that functions on behalf of fewer and fewer people, the system is continuing to work for him. He has undoubtedly never had reason to reflect upon the ironic statement of Florence Nightingale, writing from the Crimea to England in the nineteenth century: "I am not certain as to the purpose of a hospital," wrote the lady, "but I am fairly certain that a hospital is not meant for the spreading of disease." Mr. Nixon, I venture to say, has never had reason to seek medical aid in a hospital that was, in fact, dedicated to the spreading of disease —I speak of the public wards of most city hospitals today. No, if he or his family require medical attention, they get it promptly and expertly. To extend the matter, if his family seeks a school they find one; given their suppositions about education, it will be a good one. If they need the services of the courts or the law, its skills will immediately bend in their direction. They are, as their photos convey, people of health and well-being, well-housed, well-fed, well-policed, well-churched, well-armed against the stings and arrows of fate.

Many Americans, however, and the majority of men throughout the world, are not so armed, not so housed, not so fed, not so spoken for by church and state. Throughout the world, medical aid does, in fact, spread disease (either by its ineptitude or its grievous absence). Most men on earth are ill-housed, ill-fed, ill-clothed; and if to break out of this noose of despair they transgress the law, the law closes the noose with a jerk, and those who are dying slowly, die in a moment.

The point of all this, it seems to me, is a perception of our relationship to this total world scene. Given the fact that the American machine is not working well, either in its inner gears, or in its meshing with the world, good men must take action. Some of them, in the practical order of events, must be willing to go to jail, rather than to remain good citizens at large. That is to say, they must be willing to respond to what they see when they look at the machine, when they hear it misfiring, when they see human blood staining its gears. The machine has been programmed to dump out of one spigot a vast arsenal of lethal military junk (80.5 billion dollars in the current budget for war and war preparation), out of another, a diminishing trickle of services (some 11 billion dollars for all health, education, and welfare services). Someone, as a strict requirement of sanity and logic, must be willing to say a simple thing: "The machine is working badly." And if the law of the machine, a law of military and economic profit enacted by generals and tycoons, must be broken in favor of the needs of man, let the law be broken. Let the machine be turned around, taken apart, built over again.

Let the irrational power that set it to its evil production be made to listen to reason.

A few years ago, most of us of the Catonsville Nine had not thought so harshly about our social machinery. I, for one, had never before May 1968 violated a civil law. This was one experience that the nine defendants shared in common. From Guatemala to North Vietnam to Africa to the inner cities of New York, New Orleans, Washington, Newburgh, and Baltimore we had kept the law, had worked within the law, had believed that change was possible through the law. For many years we had believed that being good Americans was an acceptable secular task; within it we could work out our vocation as Christians.

But suddenly, for all of us, the American scene was no longer a good scene. It was, in fact, an immoral scene, corrupted by a useless and wasting war abroad, and a growing, petrifying racism at home. Ours was a scene that moral men could not continue to approve if they were to deserve the name of men. The American scene, in its crucial relationships—the law, the state, the Church, other societies, our own families—was placed in mortal question. Quite a charge, quite an indictment! Indeed, the change we underwent was so devastating that one misses the point entirely if he sees the Catonsville act as merely a protest against this or that aspect of American life. Catonsville, rightly understood, was a profound "No" aimed not merely at a federal law that protects human hunting licenses. Our act was aimed, as our statement tried to make clear, at every major presumption underlying American life today. Our act was in the strictest sense a conspiracy; that is to say, we had agreed together to attack the working assumptions of American life. Our act was a denial that American institutions were presently functioning in a way that good men could approve or sanction. We were denying that the law, medicine, education, and systems of social welfare (and, above all, the military-paramilitary styles and objectives that rule and overrule and control these others) were serving the people, were including the needy, or might be expected to change in accord with changing needs, that these could enlist or embody the resources of good men—imagination, moral suppleness, pragmatism, or compassion. We were denying that any major structure of American life was responding seriously on behalf of the needs of young people, of black people, of poor people, of working people, of Church people, of passionate people—as such men scrutinized their institutions, rightly expecting decent perform-ances of them.

We dared a great deal, as it turned out. We attacked an under-lying, optimistic, unassailably stubborn presupposition: that the American instance is in fact a good example of the way civilized men conduct themselves; the supposition that domestically, Ameri-can institutions serve as a model for human assembly, for dis-pensing justice, medical services, religious needs, the needs of the poor.

And in attacking the American assumption, we were beyond any doubt attacking the law and its practitioners. We were attack-ing the assumption that lawyers are capable of embodying a legal tradition and of serving us. We were attacking the assumption that American law, in its present form, can represent us, mediate our sense of justice, judge our actions, punish us.

So our act was in fact dangerous to a point that society promptly recognized. It was dangerous, as evidence of health must always be a danger to neurotic anxiety, illness, dread of life, despair, acedia, fear. Believe me, the burning of draft files by men and women like us is a kind of preliminary and particular judgment. It has to do with the end of a long patience. Which is to say, when people like us grow conscious of the fact that the jails and the courts are a necessary other end of our Vietnamese folly, then places of power and those who occupy them are indeed in danger. Men who share from birth the benefits of American life, do not commonly turn against their peers so quickly, so unequivocally. Neither kooks nor hippies nor rabid blacks, but imagine! Straight clergy, middle class, white, religious men and women—what's hap-pening, anyway?

I have perhaps suggested enough of the implications of Catons-ville, both to reassure and to shatter. To reassure: We were aiming at the law. To shatter: We were aiming beyond the law. We aimed at a social change, in a time of paralysis and dread; our hope was modest and thoughtful. We were not asking for an apocalyptic, overnight change in the character of the law of the land. We were demanding, believe it or not, no more than a minimal observance of the laws that stood upon the books. We were asking lawyers and judges for a minimal insistence on obedience to that law. We were insisting that if those in high places obeyed the law, there would be no reason for us to break the law. We were asking for a President who would obey the mandate that had given him office. We were asking for police forces that would eschew violence as their primary tactic. We were demanding that citizens accept the law of the land with regard to equal access to education and housing and jobs, for all, white or black.

Our hopes were modest. But in the rapid explosions of public fury since 1954, our hopes one by one were dashed. Law and order were violated almost universally. They were violated first of all and most frequently by those who cried to us as a slogan of social salvation, "Law and order!" The citizenry were racist, the police were violent, the Congress was delinquent, the courts were conniving, the President was expanding an undeclared war. It went on and on, an interlocking dance of death, a celebration of horror.

Then we resolved to act. The facts of the action I have described earlier; its outcome is before the courts.

I conclude on a word of hope. Our lives are part of a vast social paradox; the affluent are often eaten by secret despair, yet those who place their lives and good names in jeopardy are lit by an inextinguishable joy and hope. Indeed, we have such strong hope in the power of life, and in the vitality of our society, as to test our lives rigorously at the hands of power. We wish indeed to discover whether or not our society is dying in its main parts, or whether some mysterious new man is being born. Our act was the kind of surgical probe of which the poet T. S. Eliot speaks: "In order to be healed, our illness must grow worse."

From a certain point of view we have worsened the public condition of things. We have embarrassed good men, among them our own friends and associates in the university and in the Church. We have hardened the hearts of many who seemed to be softening toward ideals of peace and domestic justice. But such a hope would only be another form of illusion, unless it were exploring the secret and unadmitted recesses of despair and illness, which are the other side of national optimism.

So be it. We have tried to underscore with our tears, and if necessary with our blood, the hope that change is still possible, that Americans may still be human, that death may not be inevitable, that a unified and compassionate society may still be possible. On that hope we rest our case.

Five

THE WORD AS LIBERATION

Christians do not search the scriptures for the sake of justifying their life or law of conduct, for even the devil, we are told, finds words of comfort in God's word. The saying is a salutary one. The motive that drives us back to our sources is a far different one from that of pride; we go to this word in fear and trembling, knowing that the word itself is a judgment, a two-edged sword, as Paul declares. The logos is still a crisis; that is, the word is not meant to offer comfort to the slovenly, to blur the edge of life, to set up a no-man's-land in which we are free to wander at will, pursuing our pagan adventures unhindered.

The word of God is one of crisis. It confronts men, putting their acts under the scrutiny of the God of history, there to be judged. We are familiar with this. We know, too, that out of submission to God's word issue the deepest streams of joy, that this word liberates us from pharisaism, fear, dread of life, the multiple power of death in this world.

But even this is not the deepest meaning of His word to us. That meaning, I take it, is bound up with history and this world, to the degree that His word becomes our own—that we recognize in the Bible our own people, speaking our own tongue, prophets and saints, men and women who lived to the depths the common life of man, with all that implies for our own darkest hours. And finally: The word that comes to us is the mysterious voice of a brother and friend, God's Son, living our life, beckoning to us from the common condition—marketplace, family, courtroom, garden, agony, and death itself.

God's word thus urges forward and extends the range of our human experience. In its light, moreover, all suppositions about what it is to be religious, all self-justification and self-reliance, all obscene olympianism based on technology, race, and religion itself, are confronted and defeated.

One of these invitations of His word—into exodus, into freedom, into death—one scarcely knows how to characterize it—comes to us toward the end of John's gospel. The Lord is summoned into a courtroom, as He declares, to give testimony of the truth. The truth itself is on trial. It must not be presumed, before the fact, that God is speaking the truth; so men say, so the human powers decree. God must submit to the probing of man. It is for God to render account of Himself. So He answers the summons; the docket of Jesus Christ is opened before His fellows.

And this is no mock trial. Its outcome may possibly grant him new prestige, a new and cleansed people, grateful for the truth He has vindicated in the breach. Or the trial may hand Him over to death.

We know that in fact the second outcome occurred. The Lord was convicted and died the death of a malefactor. But more to our point, I would think, is the extraordinary self-conscious and deliberate manner in which the Lord entered upon the courtroom scene, and made it His own scene. He steeled himself for the crisis, He added a cubit to His stature. So that out of Pilate's court come some of the most profound and disturbing of His self-revelations. Consider, for instance: *For this have I been born, for this have I come into the world, to bear witness to the truth.* I suggest to you that the life of Jesus would have lacked something of its majesty and strength had He not stood in the court of Pilate and endured the proceedings there. I suggest, moreover, that we are offered during the trial of Jesus an example that reappears constantly and mysteriously throughout history, at the edge of life and death where the martyrs walk and let their blood. That is to say, the truth is never fully itself apart from the conditions of witness; to be itself, the truth must be summoned to accounting by the powers and dominations. It must endure crisis, it must be purified in the furnace of this world. It is not enough to declare, "I embody the truth," or "I speak the truth." Indeed, such claims are historically very nearly useless. They fall together with innumerable other such claims into the common wastebin of time. Every malcontent and charlatan and quack has claimed the truth. But the range of risk is narrowed, the issue is met, when one testifies under pressure, amid danger, to the sovereignty of a truth that he does not claim or pre-empt but that literally possesses him.

It is necessary above all to be concrete when we speak of these things. Men, even good men, are commonly disposed to submit to the slavery of the actual; they literally cannot imagine themselves in any life situation other than the one in which they live. They inherit a style, a culture, a religion—and they prolong such forms—because they are there; useful, comfortable, logical, venerable. Their minds wear the costumes of their ancestors, a clothing that was once befitting, literally, but is now simply a folklore or a fakeout. So they call a folklore a religion and a fakeout an adult life. And, alas, who shall disenchant them? But let it at least be said, as the Lord implies from His Roman courtroom, such lives as these must not make large claims to the truth.

We can think, for example, of the differing styles of truth offered by Pope Pius XI and Gandhi. They were contemporaries; both were deeply troubled by the course of events; both urged peace on the world. But one man knew at firsthand prison and fasts and marches, the immediate anguish of the masses. When he spoke, he spoke from the villages, the impoverished homes, the prisons—which are conditions of the common life of men in struggle. The other spoke from a baroque palace in the Eternal City. Today, though his words remain unimpeachable, and his tomb is honored, he is all but forgotten. Gandhi's ashes are scattered to the sea, but his words and examples are among the few spiritual legacies that survive the horrors of the past thirty years.

You may recall (we are speaking of witness and the truth)

that in 1934 Gandhi was voyaging to England to plead the cause of the freedom of the Indian masses. Pius XI refused to receive him in audience, and Winston Churchill referred to Gandhi contemptuously in Commons as "that half-naked savage." But Gandhi went on to Britain to live among the very people whom his boycott in India was threatening—the mill workers of Liverpool and Birmingham. He moved through their streets, explaining to the people in the simplest possible terms that the cause of the Indian weavers and of the British factory workers was the same cause. And they understood, and gave him a tumultuous welcome, though their own livelihood had been placed in jeopardy by Gandhi's boycott.

Now, when a man consents to live and die for the truth, he sets in motion spiritual rhythms whose outward influences are, in the nature of things, simply immeasurable. I take the courts as one symbol of Gandhi's method. What indeed did he hope for, from that vantage point? He hoped to say to others something that had come to have the deepest meaning for himself. Out of a virile disregard for personal danger and stress, he wished to make it possible for others to live—to be conscious, to be freed of demons, to welcome their brothers. The point, I would think, for Gandhi and Jesus, is not that men would agree with them, or do the same things they did. The point is that others would come to a deepened consciousness; that their sense of existence and human issues would be sharpened to the point where they would "do their thing"—a good thing, a human thing, as they were doing theirs.

The eminent scholar, C. H. Dodd, writing of Christ before Pilate, says:

It is significant that the words we are considering, on witnessing to the truth, are placed in the context of a trial scene. Where the truth is, *there* men are judged, and it is only the "man who does the truth" who can stand the scrutiny of the light. So here, John treats the question of judgment with typical irony. The Pharisees had sat in judgment on the claims of Jesus and in the end found the tables turned on them; so here Pilate believes himself to be sitting in judgment on Jesus; yet it is himself who is revealed as judged.

Americans who can bear equably with the sight of burning children are enraged and baffled by the sight of burning draft files. Moreover, Americans in the seventies are unable to create new forms of civilized political power to express our tardy sense that a bad war is being waged with our money, in our name, by our sons. We have declared a moratorium on radical or disobedient protest, and have placed our hopes, with a certain despair, in the promise of three successive Presidents to control, mitigate, and end the war. Meantime peace talks opened in Paris; but Americans and Vietnamese in enormous numbers continued to lose their lives. Our political future is clouded, to say the least; it may well be that the next years will rest in the hands of those who believe that Vietnam has established a virtuous norm of international conduct, that despite its cost, it justifies further military adventuring.

After more than four years of struggle, perplexity, and doubt, my own course is at last clear. In a sense, I claim a certain sorry advantage over most of those who have yet to choose the place and time of their response to American violence, a response that will embody their existence and carry their lives captive, in bonds to a choice, in a direction they cannot yet know. Such an hour as Catonsville may still come to them—we have every reason to believe that the price of peace will escalate grievously in the months ahead. And nothing in our history makes such a prospect easily bearable.

We have assumed the name of peacemakers, but we have been, by and large, unwilling to pay any significant price. And because we want the peace with half a heart and half a life and will, the war, of course, continues, because the waging of war, by its nature, is total—but the waging of peace, by our own cowardice, is partial. So a whole will and a whole heart and a whole national life bent toward war prevail over the velleities of peace. In every national war since the founding of the republic we have taken for granted that war shall exact the most rigorous cost, and that the cost shall be paid with cheerful heart. We take it for granted that in wartime families will be separated for long periods, that men will be imprisoned, wounded, driven insane, killed on foreign shores. In favor of such wars, we declare a moratorium on every normal human hope—for marriage, for community, for friendship, for moral conduct toward strangers and the innocent. We are instructed that deprivation and discipline, private grief and public obedience are to be our lot. And we obey. And we bear with it—because bear we must—because war is war, and good war or bad, we are stuck with it and its cost.

But what of the price of peace? I think of the good, decent, peace-loving people I have known by the thousands, and I wonder. How many of them are so afflicted with the wasting disease of normalcy that, even as they declare for the peace, their hands reach out with an instinctive spasm in the direction of their loved ones, in the direction of their comforts, their home, their security, their income, their future, their plans—that five-year plan of studies, that ten-year plan of professional status, that twenty-year plan of family growth and unity, that fifty-year plan of decent life and honorable natural demise. "Of course, let us have the peace," we cry, "but at the same time let us have normalcy, let us lose nothing, let our lives stand intact, let us know neither prison nor ill repute nor disruption of ties." And because we must encompass this and protect that, and because at all costs—at all costs—our hopes must march on schedule, and because it is unheard of that in the name of peace a sword should fall, disjoining that fine and cunning web that our lives have woven, because it is unheard of that good men should suffer injustice or families be sundered or good repute be lost—because of this we cry peace and cry peace, and there is no peace. There is no peace because there are no peacemakers. There are no makers of peace because the making of peace is at least as costly as the making of war—at least as exigent, at least as disruptive, at least as liable to bring disgrace and prison and death in its wake.

Consider, then, the words of our Savior—Who speaks to us gravely, with the burden of His destiny heavy upon Him, perplexed as we are, solicitous of heart, anxious with a kind of merciless compassion—that we comprehend lucidly, joyously, the cost of discipleship:

> You have heard it said to men of old, you shall not kill, whoever kills be liable to judgment. But I say to you that every one who is angry with his brother shall be liable to judgment.
>
> You have heard it said, an eye for an eye and a tooth for a tooth. But I say to you, do not resist one who is evil. But if any one strike you on the right cheek, turn to him the other also.
>
> Blessed are you when men revile you and persecute you and utter all kinds of evil against you falsely on my account. Rejoice and be glad, for your reward is great in heaven, for so men persecuted the prophets who were before you.

And finally,

> Pilate said to him, You are a king, then? Jesus answered, You say that I am a king. For this was I born, and for this have I come into the world, to bear witness to the truth. Everyone who is of the truth hears my voice.

Six

THE KINGDOM OF JUSTICE

The idea of judgment recurs so often in New Testament thought, one cannot but conclude that it is essential to the Lord's vision of life. Judgment. It is lodged in the Bible, lodged in the mind of Christ uneasily, even fretfully, like a foreign body in a human eye.

Christ knew the Old Testament thoroughly; the prophets were His strong meat. Those prophets had summoned the leaders of Israel to judgment again and again. David was not immune from their burning cries of justice, nor was Solomon, nor any of the great. Again and again, the prophets intervened to loosen streams of vituperation, scorn, and reproach upon the mighty. The prophets were the voice of God outraged, the voice of the poor violated. They could not endure that the will of God should be put to naught, that the defenseless should go without a hearing, that a false peace should seize upon public life and defame that kingdom of justice that was their task, their hope, their vision.

It was such nourishment as this that fed the mind of Christ as He took His destiny in hand. Men, He declared, are summoned to judgment. There is One Who sees and judges. Judgment belongs to the Father. Judges, just and unjust, are themselves to be judged. Indeed, the end of things, the last day, transforms the universe into a court of law in the image of the Sanhedrin. "When the Son of Man will come in His glory, surrounded by all the angels, He will take His place before the throne of glory.

Before Him will be assembled all the nations. He will separate them one from the other."

You are familiar with the rest. In a scene of great majesty, the Judge proceeds to His business. Some are vindicated and rewarded, others are condemned and banished.

In a sense, of course, the scene is no more than the universal drama of conscience, played out on the public stage. Long before the end, men have already judged themselves. In a thousand secret, shameful, heroic, visible ways they have met the crises that stood in their path, their hero's or rake's progress. Men have chosen for or against themselves, for or against their brothers, for or against life itself. In power and powerlessness, in fear and trembling, in joy and steadfastness, in the state of grace and the state of damnation, men have created or dismembered the world. So the scene of the end of things must be understood as being continuous with the process of things. It is within life itself, and by the living, that the living are judged. And if at a certain point of universal history the Lord intervenes and summons mankind to judgment, it is only to validate a process, already long under way, as ancient as the history of mankind itself.

Ideally, one must insist that Christians welcome the judgment of God upon their lives. Another way of saying, as I take it, that they love their Book and honor their Lord. They open their Bibles somewhat in the way they walk into their world. The world is a recognition scene, it is their geography and their native air. And then, in a contrary rhythm, they assemble, apart from their world, to hear a word of recognition, to be healed and forgiven, to recover and remember, to stand once more against the amnesia, the racism, the death-dealing, the legalized murder, the folly and waste of life, which is to say, they came together to stand against the common life, the order of business, the predictable conduct of American society.

Christians welcome judgment, even as they welcome the Lord, into Whose hands all judgment is given. In accord with this mind, I will welcome the judgment of my fellow Christians—on my life, my sins, my lovelessness, my intemperate speech, my lassitude and fear. And especially I welcome a liturgy that allows me a Christian hearing.

The fires that nine of us lit in Baltimore are hardly cool; that episode is still molten. It is part of a history that is still hot to the touch. Indeed, there is no test as yet, apt to be applied to that act. Was it timely, was it absurd; a moment of genius or of despair? We must read as we run, we must make our history even as we live it. For we do not stand at the end of things. The Lord of history, there present in all His majesty, is today somewhat in the position of a lawbreaker, his "case" still under judgment. He is variously declared dead or banished or irrelevant or, at the least, absent. So he and we must make do, all of us, acting manfully, judging and being judged; as one prisoner said in Hitler's jail, "Acting somewhat in the world as though God did not exist."

A bleak prospect indeed. We live, in truth, in this world, this society, this courtroom, in a kind of moral slum town, across the tracks from our past. We are as a people even underprivileged, certainly underdeveloped, uneasy, internecine, itching for violence, yielding like beasts to the itch, our radar scanning the four winds for imaginary enemies, our rockets ready for the leap, our inner cities savage with despair, our encircling cities also savage with despair. A scene of judgment indeed.

Indeed, it is our scene. But may we insist, Christian to Christian, that a church is not a federal courtroom, that Christians do not sit as a federal prosecuter or civil judge? Another way of insisting that our faith is not our culture, that our civil citizenship is different from our membership in Christ's Body, that Christians, by every presumption known to the Bible, have other ways than most men of judging one of their fellows. You may indeed search my heart, but you know also that there is One Who searches all hearts.

Let us then question one another as though indeed we were questioning something other than guilt before civil courts. Let us question our self-understanding, our understanding of Christ and of our world. Is it even possible that, in virtue of our common faith, you may hear from me, and I may gain from you, a far different testimony than that which will be admissible in the Federal Court of Baltimore.

Did you then perform the act of which the state accuses you? I did.

You are then guilty of the crime, as outlined in the indictment? I am not so guilty.

How can this be? You admit the acts, and you deny your guilt? Exactly.

Explain, then.

Gladly. My defense, as far as fellow Christians are concerned, is something like this. A great world power is grown distracted in mind and gigantic in pretension. The nation is fearful of change, racist, violent, a Nero abroad in the world. It seeks, moreover, to legitimatize its crimes. It stifles dissent, co-opts protests, orders its best youth into military camps, where methods of murder exhaust the curriculum. Most Christians accede to the orders. Many do so with sore hearts, most are convinced of the necessity of right reason and patience, and they say, "Let us work and wait toward better days."

But some cannot wait while the plague worsens. They confront Caesar's stronghold, his induction centers, his troop trains, his supply depots. They declare that some property has no right to existence—files for the draft, nuclear installations, slums and ghettos. They insist, moreover, that these condemned properties are strangely related one to another—that the military invests in world poverty, that Harlem and Hanoi alike lie under the threat of the occupying and encircling power.

These things being so, some Christians insist that it is in rigorous obedience to their Lord that they stand against Caesar and put his idols to the torch. They say, moreover, that it is not they who are guilty—it is Caesar. It is not they who must answer for crimes against humanity—it is he. It is not they whom the unborn will abominate—it is he.

And what of us? What of us, your fellow Christians?

There is One Who judges you and me. It is the Lord. Christ

indeed is no absentee, no dead God, no irrelevant man. *There is* One Who judges you and me. And I say in His name that your lives also are in the breach. Your justification is not assured. You, like most Christians, count on many things that before the just One count literally for nothing. You count on your prestige, your pride of place, your income, your white skin, your good repute. You walk consciously in the pride of great universities, a great people, a great society.

But there is a dark side to your moon. Most of your lives are compounded with the support of a racist society, you pay taxes to Caesar's legions as they range the world seeking whom to devour. The university makes money where it can and asks few questions, whether from war-making government or war-making industrialists. The university is no stranger to systems that insure local poverty, inflate rents, grow rich on iniquitous economic arrangements.

So living, you rejoice in your god, who is a strange being indeed —strangely American, strangely white, strangely affluent, strangely racist, strangely violent, strangely wedded to the powers that devour the poor, neglect the needy, and imprison the resister.

And yet, and yet, the true God judges you and me and our works. "I am God Almighty; you shall not have strange gods before me."

Seven

THE SPEECH DEFINES
THE STYLE

I suggest for reflection two typical days in America. The first, a ritual hunt and a ritual slaughter of beef, pork, and lamb, slain, quartered, and dressed. The event was entirely legal from start to finish. An open season was declared; the chase was on for small-size animals against whom hunting licenses had been issued. That day, we touted up more carcasses than the other team.

The war game. It was duly reported in the national press, together with a more or less precise account of the outcome, like this: "Man versus beast, man wins again." Also, a more or less vague account of the cost to ourselves, like this: "Beast versus man; beast exacts toll." Consult your local paper.

The second was less typical; it recurs only once in every four years, the inauguration day of our President. This time, no less than two Bibles were in use, no less than six clergymen thanked the Almighty, each in the accents of his own tradition, that He was our God, that we were His people.

Why not, after all? A recent survey (that last refuge of infirm minds) was conducted among the peoples of ten nations. It queried them as to their belief in God. The Americans emerged first. First even in this; they are the most consistently believing people in the world. In excess of 90 percent of them expressed belief in the Deity. Such a report must boggle the mind. According to a theology as sound as the dollar, God is safe; He is believed in, massively, by the greatest of peoples. Surely then He is to be

congratulated for such a people, for their leader, for those religious spokesman who, echoing the faith of millions, formed a
shield of truth and constancy around our new President.

There will be those who discern in the foregoing description
of recent happenings a large dose of irony. Indeed, you are correct. On many days irony itself is no defense. I flee the news
as though I had passed dangerously close to a plague-ridden
dwelling and caught a whiff of the charnel house. I walk the
gorges of Cornell in solitude, healed momentarily by the sound
of waters and the damp earth beneath my feet. I seek something,
so simple a thing as—sanity. For I confess to you that I regard
these people, who are my people, with a growing horror, this
believing nation that sounds its prayers while it goes about the
task of Cain. I hear a rhetoric from the White House, from the
cathedrals, from the new leadership and the old. And I cannot
trust it, I cannot translate it, I can barely cope with it. A leader
of my own Church returns from the latest Christmas visit to our
troops, camped like marauding buccaneers on the promontories
of the world. This gentleman returns to invoke our greatness, to
assure God's blessing on—what? If the simple truth were told, on
more of the same. More of war, more of war preparation, more
of socialized death.

The new President took the oath of office with his hand on a
Biblical passage that spoke of the transforming of weapons into
tools. It is a version of the day of the Lord, on which man
will undergo a genetic change; from warmaker to builder of his
world and his community. Bear with me while I quote the passage;
it is the word of God. "They shall beat their swords into plowshares and their spears into pruning hooks. Nations shall not lift
up sword against nation, neither shall they learn war any more."

The prophet indeed. For a commentary on the Biblical text,
let us look at the national budget for the coming year as announced by the outgoing President. Total military spending in
this year of 1969 will reach $81.5 billion dollars, exceeding the
peak of World War II. Included is provision for research on missiles that can be hidden on the ocean floor; a new generation

of missiles with multiple warheads; three new nuclear attack sub-marines; advanced bombers; carrier planes to get troops quickly to trouble spots; fast-deployment logistic ships to replace foreign bases. If one or another people grow restless under our presence, we will have heavy equipment ready offshore anywhere for our troops, after the C-5A transport planes get them to the vicinity. And so on and so on.

Seventy-two percent of the national budget is now allocated to war or war preparation. And this in a year when peace talks on Vietnam are under way. An ever larger percentage of this enormous budget is allocated, in view of the envisioned end of the current war, in the direction of further war research. By way of contrast, some 11 percent of the national budget is marked for the development of sectors of health, education, and welfare. "It is said," declares so sober a commentator as Senator George McGovern, "that in the next four years, the annual military budget will climb to over one hundred billion dollars." Thus far the beating of swords into plowshares.

I am concerned with so simple a thing as language. I am concerned with the American assumption, which indeed is one historic moment in the human assumption, that God speaks in the world, that He judges the political directions, the cultural forms, the presence or absence in men of compassion, truth, and wisdom. I believe that I am a literate man. I once learned to read, by following words on a page, somewhat as a silkworm follows the tegument of a leaf, eating as it goes. First subject, then verb, then object. The Bible helped me to read. "God said: Let there be light," or again, "Christ turned to His friends: Blessed are the makers of peace." And on another day: "Woe to you hypocrites." And finally, a speech about human speech: "Let your words be simply yea and nay."

In the assumption that God speaks to us there is implied, I believe, responsibility for right use of language or wrong. The Lord is, of course, conscious of this; He knows, moreover, all the diversity and subtlety possible to man's verbal exchange with man. In this lifetime, He experiments with the broad possibilities of verbal gestures. Now He beckons His friends into a corner, now He invites them into the public scene. Again, He enters into the grandeur of silence, turning His back upon the populous world, in favor of a desert experience. Once more, a shattering, almost unendurable cry reaches us from the cross. He shouts, He is silent, He keeps His counsel, He upbraids and lashes out, He consoles. He is literate; He reads and speaks and is silent in the world.

So He invites His friends into the uses of speech that befit man; free speech, literal speech, words in accord with the hidden figure of things, speech that reveals the logos at the heart of the world; the embodied word whose full articulation is the task of all generations of man.

In speech, the Greeks said, man is most like to the gods.

But I think we have almost reversed that claim; and here is the nub of my argument. For the Christian, as for all men living, truthful speech is a rare achievement, almost generally despaired of in a welter of public conflict, ambition and pain, the onslaught of bestial forces that tear our soul from our body, the enticements to violence, the subjugation of the mind before the dark powers of dread, fear, lust, and envy.

From this it occurs that outrages of the basest sort are normalized behind a façade of politesse. Life goes its course, even while it were better named death. The isolation of power separates men more and more from the fate of victims.

"I did not know," said a character in a novel of Camus, "that for years my father, an austere, impeccable man, used to rise early on certain days. I knew he held an office called something like public prosecuter. I only learned later that he went regularly in the morning to attend the hangings of those he had condemned." (*The Stranger*)

The father hastened to the hanging as though to a holiday. It was the bitter, logical end, as the boy came to understand, of the obscene work of condemning one's brothers. Indeed, hangings go on; they are a form of crime common to all men. The Greek pagans realized as much; their tragedies tell us so. Blood has always been let, sons have killed fathers, wives were unfaithful, kings were slain by spouses, a father gouged out his eyes, a mother slew her children and scattered their bones before her pursuing husband. Blood was let, the tragedies were steeped in blood. But such action was strictly, from a dramatic point of view, obscene; *ob scaenum*, banished, forbidden the stage, Such abominations such shady business, could only occur offstage, somewhere in the wings.

But what happens to a man who lets the blood of another man? This was the real question, the tragic question. The question of bloodletting was not, from the point of view of the tragic vision, interesting at all. But the question of consequences, of psychic change, of the corruption of man's spirit, this was very nearly the only question worth asking. Then and now, it is very nearly the only question worth asking; worth asking of the military, of the paramilitary society of militarized Christians, of the churches militant. What happens in the heads of those who accede to bloodletting as a social method? What happens to the new mandarins, to the social managers, to the intellectuals, to the actionists, to the students when men turn toward death as a way of life?

The father hastened to a hanging, as though to a holiday. The son at length came to understand. As his father left the house in the darkness before dawn, the child arose, a child no more, a man. He was son of his father, but he was a stranger to his father. The difference was a simple one, and yet it made all the difference. It made the son a new man, it set him apart from all those who went before, who attended hangings, who condemned their brothers. It set the boy apart from those who held power, from those who sent other men to prison and hastened to their death. A new understanding aligned the boy with those who had no part in that scene, who abominated the scene. It set him apart from those who inhabited it, who named it the real world and made a human shambles of it, and then bequeathed it to their sons. Perhaps those fathers would live to hear their sons say, "The life you have opened before us is a lie, an abomination. We turn our backs on it."

Obscene. A major portion of public speech, embracing as it does death for its method, recommending destruction and division as invaluable social tools, is in the strictest classical sense, obscene speech. It is irresponsible and conniving, a speech of murderers. Such speech, in violation of the Greek canons, is nonetheless spoken upon the center stage, is rendered plausible, is proven effective, is technologized, multiplies its victims by the thousands. It borrows from social engineers and social scientists its corrupt legitimacy, it flies in the face of tradition, of reason, of the laborious, millennial task of civilizing man, it tears apart the fabric of health, imagination, conscience, and faith, it perverts trust, it drags the conscious universe backward into the slime of the irrational and unmanageable. And all the while, such speech, seduced and seducing, drowns the simple, lucid words by which man once reached outward to his brother, forged his art, reflected on his experience, made love.

In the name of the Gospel, I condemn today the speech of power politics, the speech of military murder, the language of religious mystification, all language that indicates the death of the mind, the studied obscenity, the speech that pretends to human dignity and truth while in fact it brings down the world.

And I recommend in the name of the Gospel, modesty and loyalty, the springs in the desert; all the hidden efforts of men to live with human difference, to bear with crisis, to bind up wounds, to be patient and long-suffering.

I suggest, nay, I *insist* that the gospel language condemns our usual language, that discipleship reproves once and for all our intolerable inflation of spirit, that the yea and nay of the Gospel is impatient before our studied prevarications; finally, that the powerlessness of Jesus is of greater moment than the powers and dominations in whom we commonly trust.

Ob scaenum. Obscene. The speech defines the style. The speech of the sons judges the lives of the parents. The obscenity of the sons is purer than the hypocrisy of the parents. The peacemaking of the sons is more acceptable than the warmaking of the parents.

If then you seek a clue, grow humble and listen to your sons.

For they have cast off the filthy burden of your original sin. Rather than kill their brothers, they go into exile or prison. They leave your houses desolate, your churches empty. They judge that in such a world as you bequeath to them, they must die rather than murder, suffer rather than inherit.

I close with a story whose translation into life I leave in your hands.

A gathering was held within the last year in Mexico, consisting of some twenty persons from the peace communities of North America. The question arose at a certain point: "What makes a man peaceable?" The question had been intensely discussed for some time, with one of the participants remaining silent. Finally, when he was pressed as to his thought, he remarked simply, "I believe there is enough latent violence in this room to begin a war."

A long and somewhat shocked silence followed. Could it be true, each one was thinking, that in his heart, which he had fancied was the heart of a peacemaker, there lay the unexorcised will to murder? The thought was disturbing and portentous.

The silence then was broken by a second question addressed to the same speaker. "If this is indeed true, then what is required in order to stop a war?"

And the same silent man spoke again, in his direct and simple fashion. "You know, I think that someone would be required to die."

Eight

EXIT THE KING AND
CRISIS OF AMERICA

The war indeed has been a long loneliness. It has brought us too much knowledge and little consolation, too much protest, too little joy. We know too much about Vietnam, too much about American moral savagery, too much about hedonists, too much about puritans, too much about polltakers, taxpayers, and warmakers. So much indeed that we must begin again to unwind and unlearn, to waste many hours, if we are to have anything new to offer the times. It is necessary that some, perhaps even wasting time, will become contemplatives, that is to say, men of profound and available sanity. Some of us may also become madmen—men who have the courage, like Simon and Garfunkel, to "look for America." Some of us may even become inspired activists—a way perhaps of combining the above-mentioned ventures in one fresh genetic package.

As one man's offering out of ignorance and waste, I want to reflect upon an extraordinary French myth. And I want to suggest, not being too earnest about the use of time, and drawing upon the resources of another man's imagination, that we may even become literate. By that I mean that the universe and reality itself may become an available text for a civilized community. And I venture even to offer an apologia for such a method; to suggest that in fact most Americans are illiterate, in a sense that is both literal and lamentable. Fully four-fifths of our two hundred million fellow citizens—beginning with the men who wield power over us, and continuing through the universities, the legal institutions, and the churches—are simply illiterate.

Let me try to illustrate what I mean. Before the military coup of 1964, Brazilian educators had launched an exciting literacy campaign, destined, with one stroke and in a single generation, to open the text of the world before the disintegrated consciousness of the peasants. These men, to many of whom I spoke, called their experiment "conscientization"—the process and act of growing conscious. I am suggesting that we speak of our fellow Americans in an exactly equivalent way, and of the necessity of a like act and process. I am suggesting that most Americans, especially those who claim authority over others, are unconscious (in the Freudian sense of the word), with all the revenge and destructiveness implied by deliberate regression. From another point of view, such men are simply illiterate. They are unable, in Buber's phrase, to imagine the real world. They are unable, in Simone Weil's phrase, to put on the universe for a garment. They are unable, in the Christian phrase, to "connect" with the body of man, with which we are joined member for member.

In speaking this way, one is strangely enough trying to express hope rather than despair. Hope, as we are coming to realize more fully and painfully, is a reductive virtue, even as its opposite number, despair, is inflationary—the intent of the first being honesty and contact with reality, the intent of the second being a rhetoric of deception. For the present, in our country, I venture that resources of literacy and consciousness (and these are really our hopes) are at present reduced to a few pockets of people, their eyes burning like Blake's "Tiger in the Night." A few student groups, a few groups of the poor, a few communities of black people, a few religious groups, a few professionals. These people, one would have to concede, have almost no power. Or, more closely regarded, they have drawn away from the illiterate and regressive forms that power has taken. And they are seeking new forms of power, which is to say, they are learning to read and write. And by the time they have learned to pronounce a few words and understand them—let us say, for instance, the word "man"—by that time they will have found to their unutterable astonishment something that the peasant of Brazil discovered to his: It is possible to be a man. It is possible to join "I" to the verb form "am" and then to claim for oneself everything another man claims for himself: humility, hope, tools, a morrow, housing, schooling, respect for the spirit, power, inclusive and humane policy, sane priorities in uses of the earth, ecological reverence, leisure.

But to speak more closely, it is possible that many students who have engaged in projects of human compassion, in peace work or programs combating racism, if questioned "What did you learn?" would be able to answer, "To write and read." Let the students explain their answer to a generation that has presumed to both skills, and in fact possesses neither.

In any case, to our question of literacy and Americans I should like to propose the parable of Ionesco's *Exit the King*. The play has to do with the omnipresence of death. It can, in fact, be understood as an exploration of the modes of death operating in the modern world: the death of a king, the destruction of nature, the death of wisdom, the extinction of love and enterprise and even of the power of imagining alternatives to death itself. The king is dying; and in his wake the land is folding in like a batch of dough. . . .

You know how many ways there are to die. I do too. So do the Vietnamese. So do black people. Indeed, one of the perverse triumphs of technology is to reverse the Biblical promise in favor of death: "Where life abounded, death did more abound." The improved families of antipersonnel weapons, the improved napalm, the germicides and herbicides and defoliants press upon victim peoples at home and abroad the presence of death as the prime ingredient of American consciousness.

Now I submit that the first task of a literate man is not to "face death." It is to submit to the mystery of life, a different matter altogether. And I think this is Ionesco's implication. America, that America that presumes to speak for us in the world at large, and for God as well, and for the human community at this point in history—that America is *literally illiterate* with regard to the meaning and value of life. If I stress this fact, it is not to push a moral accusation. It is merely to suggest a point, indeed, to clarify the point of conflict between war-makers and peacemakers, between racists and communitarians, between the disciples of inevitability and men of freedom, between deceivers and friends.

Ionesco helps us to understand the full horror of our predicament: death for everyone. He is suggesting first of all that the exit of the king is by implication the exit of almost everyone. All those who have put their trust in the king's methods, essentially reducible to one method, murder—all those who have aped him, served him, boot-licked him, gone along with him, come to terms with him, fought for him, made peace with him, gone to bed with him, said Mass for him; all who have been his slaves, his whores, his ministers, his generals, his priests, his men-at-arms, all these are on the way out. Exit the king, exit everyone. Without him, none of these others have any validity. They have no more place—onstage, or in the world. Death is atrociously and totally in command of modern man. And a simple device serves to dramatize the truth. At various points of the drama, certain actors disappear, with a flick of the lights. It is as though their prior existence, their dramatic content, had never been more than a fiction. So they are extinguished when the fiction is wrung dry.

With one exception. And now the obituary ends and the drama commences. Two women had helped, for good and ill, to shape the soul of the king. Marguerite, the courtesan, and the queen. The first is a woman of great beauty and attraction, the second has no beauty and no distinction, the tongue of an angry fishwife and a mind that will bear watching. Marguerite's function is one of love. She is devoted to the king and never wearies of saying so. But it soon becomes apparent, according to Ionesco, that this love is a seduction. It serves to keep alive the illusions of the king, first by assuring him that he is not going to die, and then, when that prospect becomes increasingly improbable, by the use of delaying tactics; by keeping at distance the horror and darkness of his last hours.

You may see her, as you will, as a particularly skillful hypocrite. Her character would have special overtones in France, where themes of hypocrisy are naturally drawn from an ancient religious culture. But in this country, secular Americans would perhaps recognize Marguerite as the pudding-headed lover, the anxious liberal, the middle-class mother. Her function is to paralyze change, at exactly that point where change is needed, which is to say at the depths of man's spirit. She keeps the king unconscious and illiterate, and thus infantile and possessed by others. Instead of mediating the convulsion of history to his soul, she interrupts the free flow between nature and his manhood, and so destroys him.

One cannot praise too highly this insight of Ionesco: the death function of soft-hearted and wrong-headed love. One thinks of all those mothers who keep their sons from growing up in any image but their own despair and bafflement and dread of life. One thinks of all those professors who choose, in the name of intellect, to rule out of order the issues that crowd in on their students, devouring and creating them, at the threshold of the classroom, but never within. One thinks of the death urge of mother Church: her false silence, her diluting of the facts of life, and the consequent malfunctioning of religious people in face of the brute facts of change. Indeed, Marguerite appears to me simply as pure America: the American university, the American parent, the American Church. Or perhaps you may see her as the lady on the war poster. She is shapely and chaste—and murderous. She is designed by the old to keep the death game going, by the old who have survived two games—cheap love and cheap death. See your local draft board.

I marvel at the subtle irony Ionesco offers us through Marguerite. It has to do with the avoidance of death as a fact of life, and the imposition of death as a method of change. Like the last spasm of a dying shark, the king, at her urging, is constantly ordering his few remaining subjects off to death. At her urging he is also constantly escaping himself. For Marguerite wants the king around. She wants his power, and she needs his illusions in order to possess him. She needs him, not in the way of love, which is a communion, a marriage of minds, an adventure in consciousness, a literacy test for both parties, a power that once tasted and shared, shares power and gives men a taste for freedom. Marguerite does not want the king in the way of a bride. She "wants him around" in the old careless way of the bitch-whore, who also wants poodles and bonbons. Yet her ways are so friendly and fetching that almost anybody in reading the play for the first time and seeing Marguerite operate will opt fervently for her as the king's savior and lover—which indeed she is, given our local habitation and name: America and the proliferation of false saviors and lovers.

What happens toward the end of the play? An extraordinary moment of truth. Marguerite has just declared once more, "I will always be with you, I will never leave you." And then she disappears. As simple as that. The king is left with his failing vision and his slowing heart. Now he is helpless; others must stand him up or carry him about. He is left with the queen, and himself and death. The classroom is cleared of all its toys and debris and distraction, and the king is at last ready for that lesson in literacy he had so long delayed and feared. He may at the end begin to read the universe and his own heart, and so to grow conscious.

The one who remains with him, in the shoddy throne room with its long and reaching shadows, is the queen. And she is a terror. She has grown old with the king, and though her death is only hinted at, it is fairly clear that she will not survive him. Acid of tongue and fierce of eye, she hangs around to the end. "Hangs around"; the phrase is an exact one. She is, in fact, an appendage, an arm, a nearly paralytic limb, joined to the old king, flesh and bone to flesh and bone. Married to him; or, in the old phrase, stuck with him. And like a good, long-suffering wife, she has never quite bought her husband. So she can be partner in a quarrel with life itself, she can probe his illusions, his pomposities. She has seen the king with no clothing on, she knows in fact how little manhood there is under it all. She knows that the warrior was a coward. The public figure lacked special grace, the orator was a liar, the conqueror was a killer. So she can insist on the truth, in face of the comforting lies of Marguerite. "He *is* going to die," she says again and again. "Look at him; his limbs are failing, he can't walk, he can hardly see."

Marguerite, dare we say it, is the Great Society, beautifying America, napalming Vietnam, making a buck here and there (but mostly under the table), kissing babies, taking temperature readings of the public, adapting the liberal line to the latest idiocy of the electorate, flying in from foreign wars with good news; ignorant of peacemaking and filled with talk of pacification, limiting armaments and selling arms, decrying violence and death and pushing war and death-dealing. In sum, injecting power with a mortal progressive illness of illusion and illiteracy.

And the queen? She is, in a phrase that is at once ridiculous and exact, the king's better half. Literally. Spiritually. She is that marriage he can never quite consummate and never quite be rid of. She has one great advantage, from the point of view of existence itself, an advantage that Ionesco has sensed and exploited with brilliance. Simply, she is married to the king. She has the legitimacy that natural health and truth always have over pretension and illusion. "Look at him," she says, "he *is* going to die." You understand, she is capable of the truth only. She has no beauty, nothing to offer to lust, no way out of troubles, no diplomacy, nor solutions, as the land goes sour and the children die and the armies approach. She has no theology, she cannot point out that according to several world religions death is a way of new life. No, she has only what small measure of truth she has. She is like the last peasant of her kingdom, an ignorant person whose knowledge stops with her eyes and ears. She is an agnostic; there are only one or two things she can see. The rest is off somewhere at the edge, she prefers to concentrate.

I believe that in talking of the play, we have been talking

about our subject, the crisis of America. I am suggesting that the nature of that crisis is so pervasive and mysterious that indeed I am at a loss, in discussing America and the symbols of Ionesco, to point to an outcome. Will America be capable of the resolution indicated by the play—an outcome of health, sanity, good sense, and courage? Marguerite is canceled out, the queen survives, to go on with the king, into death. With America, I need not point out that another outcome is entirely possible, indeed becomes more probable every day. That is to say, it is entirely credible that the whore will survive the queen, the illusion the truth, the unconscious the conscious, the illiterate the wisdom. I do not know. The drama is still in progress.

But I think it helpful to suggest that the king is a corporate person. There live in him all the illusions and fears and regressiveness, as well as all the possibilities, of all of us. The point, as I understand it, is an insight of Shakespeare as well as of the Bible. The king is ourselves. It is possible that many good men, or even a few, will insure the survival of the queen, of decency and truth and life itself. They do this by insuring the survival of these things in themselves. Whether we will choose to go whoring with our lives, or whether we will marry, and in so doing will accept the rigors of love and fidelity, and will grant a hearing to the truth—these choices remain crucial in the personal drama of each, and for all.

In the midst of such unresolved choices, the young, of course, have great advantage, and stand in great danger. For in the symbols of the play, it is they who are of age both for marriage and prostitution. The old men who wield power in society are, in a radical sense, capable of neither marriage nor whoring. They can only live out the shabby drama of their own early years. Their old age is a kind of long, obscene stag party; its game is essentially voyeurism; they must enlist and pay others to play the games that quicken their sluggish blood—cheap love and cheap death. So they need mercenaries and Madison Avenue; they cannot really make it—neither love nor war. They can only infect us with the illness of false normality, set a stage for a drama called, say, the "Great Society," into which they may dump all the illusions of the good life. And all the while, out there in Vietnam, out there in the ghetto, out there in the third world, out there in us, the real drama continues: death as enforceable method, military solutions, fear, nausea, extinction as a social method.

I do not know how to be more specific or more immediately helpful. You know that I have made a choice of my own; I can only hope that it favors the queen, whom the Quakers call more abstractly, "the truth which speaks to power." My brother Philip and I are sentenced to federal prison for war resistance. Church and State are officially horrified by our actions. Two of my brothers are hawkish, two nephews are fighting in Vietnam. Marguerite and the queen are contending under our own roof; a struggle for the soul of the king goes on. Our parents are living out their last years on such a scene; facing it . . . making it, I say proudly.

By way of immediate help, I can perhaps offer a kind of literacy test drawn from these reflections, attempting to deal with aspects of our own scene. You may choose to take the test or not, as you will. But I think, in any case, that the test has some bearing on a man's skill or clumsiness in reading the text of his own society—dare I say the text of his own heart?

1. Relationships are of more import than tactics. I offer this cliché with pride, knowing full well it is as old as Socrates or Jesus, and fully as ignored. But on its understanding, everything that follows, and perhaps much more, depends.

2. The validity of politicizing others as a tactic is always questionable. My difficulty is not with the tactic as such, but with the way it almost inevitably becomes an occasion for manipulation of others, on behalf of more or less laudable purposes. I suggest that the ambiguous character of such tactics can be reduced. But only if the political agent himself is being humanized by his actions.

3. Since we Americans have SEATO, NATO, OAS, Generals Park, Ky, and Westmoreland, Chiang Kai-shek, the Japanese, the

Australians, the Filipinos, we scarcely need you. *Capisch?* I am trying to say: Do not validate old, bankrupt methods of coercion and murder by creating new, bankrupt methods of roughly the same things.

4. "Doing one's thing," rightly understood, is a way of opening doors to the imagination. Naturally enough, the days being what they are, no one wants to entrust his future to diplomacy or to the military. So the saying, "Do your own thing" is one that neither Mr. Rusk, nor the average ambassador, nor the average military man can praise or emulate. But for student groups and others it has meant a very precious thing: "Among us, you are a free man. Become yourself."

5. At the same time, "Do your own thing" can be twisted by the immature and undisciplined in accord with their own whims. Then it becomes a license, a kind of big or little game hunt. Taken in this corrupt sense, a perverse and illogical and selfish activity gets under way. Activists ruin others because "their thing" demands intellectual or sexual coercion. In the name of doing a big public thing, they do shameful personal things and leave the wreckage of other lives to mark their trail—which to anyone unimpressed by their ego, is no more than a rake's progress.

6. Corrupt and current forms of power make great capital of abstract terms in order to mask their chief occupations. So men speak publicly today of "pacification" when they really mean violence and death-dealing on a large scale. They speak of "escalation," indifferently, both in regard to peace and war, when they really mean more fervent pursuit of murder or of social control. They speak of "antipersonnel activity" when they really mean civilian killing. But the rhetoric of activist groups also has its seductions and dangers. Sometimes the language masks an itch for revenge and violence, and contains nothing new, whether by way of spiritual resources or imagination. The most accurate thing that can be said about it is that it has despaired of communication.

7. Everyone with an eye in his head can recognize universal problems. This is not the task. The task is to localize the universal, to render it manageable by getting to work on it where

one lives. A downtown community center, a single good issue of a good underground paper, a neighborhood free college, these are worth a thousand manifestos on the state of the world. The real question is, "What can a few men and women offer to a few others by way of alternatives to the general, indeed universal reliance on death?"

8. The consciousness of the liberal is in principle broken in fragments. He picks one of the fragments, deals with it and thinks he is conscious. So, for instance, he thinks the end of the Vietnam war will give him a kind of magical access to the "good old days." To such a man, any war is an isolated instance, and almost any peace is good enough to settle for. But the consciousness of the radical man is integrated. He knows that everything leads to everything else. So while he works for the end of the war, for the end of poverty, or for the end of American racism, he knows also that every war is symptomatic of every other war. Vietnam to Laos and on to Thailand, and across the world to Guatemala, and across all wars to his own heart. What he is finally looking for is not a solution (knowing as he does that human history has not offered solutions). He is really working for a creation: a new man in a new society.

9. When human hope is authentic, it contains and deals with and finally overcomes a large measure of despair. When hope is illusory (that is to say, liberal), it becomes itself a form of the despair it pretended to alleviate. Compare the stature and available resources of, say, David Miller and General Hershey. David operates out of a modest assessment of spiritual and political wealth. His wife and he bear cheerfully with long separation, loneliness, and poverty. The community has pledged to support them both, and is doing so. But Hershey is conceivable only in the corrupt milieus of weekdays at the Pentagon and church on Sunday. His god has not been heard from. Neither has his community.

10. I say the following with great reserve, but say it nonetheless: Every blade requires an edge in order to follow through. That is to say: The times are such that in order that some men

be free, someone must be in jail. Think today of the prisoners who pay so much more for freedom than you do, and who perhaps understand it so much more deeply.

11. If you cannot live in the horse's mouth, you will probably never make it into the lion's den. Translation: Every activist needs a hippie at the back of his mind. Operation requires celebration. And these are merciful final words: Enjoy, enjoy!

Nine

LEAR AND APOCALYPSE

Most of us find it not at all humiliating to confess that *Lear* is far beyond us. Indeed many minds, converging throughout many centuries, have scarcely begun to absorb its grandeur and horror.

But for us perhaps, a more modest task can be envisioned. We are exploring whether or not the apocalyptic consciousness may, in this instance, be proper to old age. But more than that, whether or not apocalyptic happenings may not bring an old man to his true greatness, a man with the burdens of power and family. May not such responsibility bring on a crisis, in which his soul may stand purified and vindicated?

We begin with evidence of the distemper and frivolity of old age. The king has decided to divide his kingdom before his death —laudable enterprise indeed, since at one stroke it will erase divisions induced by the personal ambition of his successors! But he connects his decision with a strange insistence: a trial by declaration of love. He wants, for reasons that remain his own, to discover which of his three daughters loves him most. Presumably, once discovered, true love will come to its immediate reward.

It is to the eternal praise of the youngest of the daughters that she refuses to play her father's game.

She may be the first within recorded Western history to open the generation gap and look coolly at what lies within.

Is she the creator of that gap? Or was her father its engineer, in creating her? We do not, of course, know. We do know, from our own lifetime, that the young are ridden by wild horses. We know also that the day when the begetting of a child was a prospect to be contemplated with detachment is forever and stormily ended.

We are not even sure of Cordelia or of her game; we are given evidence only that her soul is well knitted, a unity. She appears on stage briefly; rumors about her have mainly to do with reverence or contempt before her suffering compassion. But she remains somewhat abstract and shadowy: She does not have the harsh texture, the immediate clamorous impact of her two sisters. *Their* projects are always clear; there is that to be said for them. But Cordelia is a little bloodless, like a Dickens heroine. We can only be grateful for her, and mourn that we cannot know her better.

Edmund is also a bane to his father. But that, according to the theology and folklore of the day, is easily explained. For Edmund is a bastard, pure and simple, whereas these three daughters have been conceived in wedlock, and are judged therefore to have their organs and wits in fair conjunction with the universe. Alas!

I like Edmund, because he refused to lay the crimes of his parent (or of himself) to the stars. No, he insists, it is men themselves who are guilty or innocent; look at his father and his own begetting. Look, if you dare, at himself.

Is the meaning of the play hidden, like a secret number or sign, in such lines as, "Nothing comes of nothing?" It may indeed also be true, and we who live may weep for it, that if nothing comes of nothing, then something will usually come of something. And the implication of the play itself is that that "something" is not always as sweet as roses, or as unlike a dragon's tooth as a grateful child.

Whether the scene in question includes the father and the daughters, or the father and a disguised loyal servant, or the father and his retinue, there is always, or almost always, the fool between. And he supplies the strongest evidence of the sanity and genius of the creator of *Lear*. For it is the fool who mediates, translates, and at times turns aside the nearly intolerable agonies that threaten to suffocate the main actors. . . .

Causes of the "generation gap" (not all of these are explored by Shakespeare):

1. Mutual selfishness
2. Mutual betrayal
3. Conflict of interests
4. Different drummers
5. Hair
6. Baldness
7. Ingratitude; "I, Lear, gave them everything."
8. Truth
9. Untruth

The three daughters are, of course, excitingly different. Cordelia illustrates what we might call the cruelty of true love. Regan and Goneril are, for us as well as for their father, instances of the softness of cruel love. Their opening speeches drip with honey, but their hearts are gall.

Lear, under the surgical hand of Shakespeare, must deal with the uses and misuses of adversity. An old man goes temporarily mad under the burden of neglect and rejection by his family. What none of his enemies and none of the pressures incidental to power could bring him to, his daughters' cruelty speedily accomplished.

But we are left wondering whether his madness was really induced by the ingratitude and betrayal of his daughters. Was he disappointed in legitimate hope, or was he betrayed by his own ego, which on every other occasion during a long life had powerfully stood by him? It is a question not only for parents, it is a question also for those whose parenthood lies ahead. The future gathers force in the quality of life now in evidence, now under experiment. If the young are selfish on principle, they are not likely to be rendered unselfish by marriage. Their selfishness is merely given a wider field of action, as they prolong an old game, dealing with their children as no more than extrapolations of their own ego.

Somewhere, in that tight and intricate web of relationships that the family creates, a man must search out the meaning of his life. And that is bound to be a bloody business—far more bloodletting than the act of love, or the act of birth.

A comparison between Job and Lear is rich in implication, and comes almost immediately to mind. Job's plaint is directed to God. He longs mightily, out of his present adversity, not to have been born at all. Lear, on the other hand, never addresses God directly; more, his verbal explosions never imply that he regrets his existence. He is always wrestling with life itself. He wishes to be, even now to choose not to be. But he would have the choice to be his own. Are we to read here a significant difference between the primitive man of power, and the man of power in sophisticated society?

The fool always asks reconciliation. In this he is a fool, by profession and personal admission. In a world in which power is exercised in the normal way, it is in the strictest sense a foolish thing to ask that men grant space to one another; to live, to rejoice, to adhere one to another. Life and the granting of life are not serious issues with most men of power, so they risk bringing down their lives and the lives of others.

Lear thought that the disposition of his kingdom was the most serious, indeed the first task of his old age. For this he is to be praised, within measure. But he is to be blamed for not going far enough. And that "not far enough" is attested to, not only by his virtuous daughter, but in fact by all three. For what all three beneficiaries longed for (in differing ways, to be sure) was the proper disposition of his heart. That was the inheritance they sought. And the denial of that turned one in the direction of heroism, and the others toward destruction and betrayal.

In Act III, Scene 2, the fool's prophecy, irony is heaped upon irony, in the fool's conception of the well-run Kingdom of Albion. That is to say, he is canny enough to know that the best common sense, applied with whatever purpose and skill, only brings greater and greater public confusion. A stroke of bitter genius! Men are literally unable to conceive, or to cope with, a kingdom in which common sense is the rule of thumb and the basis of lawful activity.

Ingratitude. Lear declares again and again, in madness and in sound health, its contrariety to nature. But the consequent travail and dislocation must also be seen, I would think, as the results of his own war against nature. Lear had been a conventional king, after all. That is to say, violence had been his ordinary method. It could not but follow that he would be a profoundly conventional parent. And while it may be true that a kingdom can be preserved by convention, the course of history has never entirely allowed that children can be dealt with, and flourish, under the same method.

The king and parent has two expectations, intermingled to the points of arrogance and folly: obedience; and gratitude. The world, by its very course, does much to correct such hopes. The vocation, then as now, remains the same; a man has a child, and is required to love that child, even when he runs wild in the world's traces.

Tragedy builds layer on layer, by inclusion of contrary ironies. Thus; nature violated and violating, fatalism and freedom, foolishness and wisdom, treachery and fidelity, madness and sanity.

A necessary condition of tragedy is an imbalance of sympathies. Lear is the protagonist from one point of view, simply because we know most about him. In order to restore things, we might need *The Tragedy of Goneril and Regan* or *The Comedy of the Third Daughter*.

But, of course, these are impossible. The creation of alternatives cannot be the function of pure tragedy. Because alternatives always introduce impurity, they are too close to actual life to work onstage.

Or is *Lear* big enough to include these other lives, to the point where we are willing to include their demands and directions?

The fool can be bawdy, even in bad weather. The king can only be tragic. And this is his tragedy.

"I am a man more sinned against than sinning." In such a sentence a whole theology is brought to bear on the unbearable. Is the true sinner, in such a case, God, or one's fellow? In any case, the admission of at least relative innocence is of the essence of life itself, lived at such pitch as this play reveals.

An apocalypse can only occur to a man conscious of a measure of goodness, a measure of openness in the face of the closure men call sin. Were a man conscious of himself only as totally depraved, could he ever summon those resources of opposition and rage that make for a moral happening? I doubt it.

Altogether, the reversal of roles seems also to be demanded. And this not as a mere matter of donning successive masks. What is involved is the dissolution and creation of the *persona*, the mask that is the very physiognomy of the soul in conflict—a change of heart, a conversion. *Hubris* can confront the gods, but it can never assimilate man with them. The king must be maddened before ever he can become sane. More; by implication he was already insane, before his state became shockingly and publicly clear. That is to say, his consciousness had been ill attuned to the laws of his own mind and to the laws of nature, revealed to him through his relationships. Perhaps this means simply that one cannot wield power for long and not be actively insane. It is, after such a long life of power, that the king comes to the factiousness and illusion of old age, recorded in the opening scene. Necessity is the handmaid of freedom; what follows must follow, if he is to be saved.

Ten

THE BOOK OF REVELATIONS

The word "apocalypse" comes from a Greek term meaning "to unveil." Thus, an apocalypse is a kind of revelation, or as Joyce would put it, an "unveiling" or "epiphany."

In the strictly religious sense, we are dealing with a word spoken by God to men. In this sense, of course, all sacred books are apocalyptic. However (and the division is not at all clear), some of these books contain strong elements of prophecy; some of them, further, are quite exuberant or baroque in their symbolic and dramatic content.

Our apocalypse of St. John is in a kind of middle ground between the Lear-like tragedy of Ezekiel and the wild, apocalyptic forms that flourish in the second century before Christ.

We have always to deal, in this literary form, with symbols. Of these, almost a recognizable glossary arose in the course of time, at least in the classical mold. For instance, eyes symbolize knowledge; wings, mobility; hands or horns, power and domination; a crown represents the royal estate of the one who carries it. A long robe symbolizes the priesthood; a palm, triumphs; a sword, destruction. So also the colors of the spectrum took on a symbolic value. White was the sign of joy, purity, and victory; blood red was the sign of martyrdom; scarlet, the sign of luxury and pomp.

There was also a constant "numbers game." Seven was the most generally used number and had always to do with perfection or fullness. Four was a sign of the created world; twelve, the sign of the new Israel.

Some ancient iconography, issuing from a simpler sensibility than our own, mingled the symbols in a way that we find disconcerting. Thus, for instance, in medieval stained glass one can see at times the enthroned Christ, with the sword issuing visibly from His mouth. For ourselves, a different tack is perhaps helpful; not to be preoccupied with the literal coherence or plastic effect of the symbols as they accumulate in the test. The symbols were simply a mode of translating the ideas that the author had received from God; they were by no means meant to communicate a vision that would be *imaginable*. Thus, for instance, it would be absurd to try to imagine visually the lamb with seven horns and seven eyes, or the beast with seven heads and ten horns. The translation must be, if one may so speak, intellectual. Thus the lamb has power and knowledge in its inner fullness. The beast represents the Roman Empire with its emperors (the heads) and its vassal kings (the horns).

Of more import by far is the vexed meaning of the *dramatic* symbols of apocalyptic literature. Their deepest meaning, of course, is one of moral movement and crisis. The symbols are borne along in a tide of history, for good or for ill. That is the stuff of the apocalypse—a vision of the beginning and of the end of things. The symbols dissolve and reassemble; they show that history is forever beginning anew, forever being crushed by illegitimate power and immoral circumstance. So men find themselves, when they are most truly men, not on some neutral no-man's-land or middle ground of life. They find themselves perpetually torn from the bowels of yesterday, forever threatened by the multiple forms of death that press upon them from this world. They spend their lives in the experience of a deathbed or of a room of birth, they scarcely know which.

It is precisely this aspect of death and life that we might call the apocalyptic element of human life and of literature.

The first is a psychological or spiritual aspect of man's experience. The second belongs more properly to his literary forms.

It is not so much that man discovers in an aprioristic way the life-death theme as pre-eminent. Rather the theme is borne in upon him by an experience of God or of this world. He knows that he stands at the beginning of things or at the end of things —or, perhaps, at both of these. For the first generation of Christians, this beginning-end view of history was induced by many facts of life. Among these, the persecution by Nero was of capital import. Such times of sudden death gave the Church a large number of martyrs, men and women whose deaths would be models for the days and centuries to come. But in a far deeper sense, this traumatic experience (which can only be compared in its impact upon sensibility with the effects of the Nazi holocaust upon the Jews) actually seeded the imagination of believers with a special sense of themselves and of the world.

It was, simply, an apocalyptic sense. It allowed Christians to see themselves as perpetually at a beginning and an end of things. The converging facts of consciousness were the teachings of Jesus about the proximity of the end of things, and the massacre of Christians. These met in the Christian imagination; so believers became acutely aware of life as a point of conflict, an inevitable juncture of the power of life and death.

It is, of course, extremely hazardous and difficult to trace the development of a given sensibility. But we are perhaps justified in suggesting that to early Christians, the imagination of Jesus was also apocalyptic. He seemed to sense not only that He would be a point of depature for countless lives, but that He would be a "sign" to be contradicted, pulled down, destroyed, remade, and lifted anew.

After so dramatic (in the strictest sense) a life as His, it is no wonder that Christians saw themselves as literally the consummation of history, with nothing to follow except the end of things —the intervention of God and the vindication of His faithful ones. The theme of glory follows upon a very special sense of time. So the Book of Revelations introduces us to time as a dramatic field of force. Time is by no means so inhuman a thing as the movement of planets relative to one another. It is rather human consciousness, heightened in view of the end of things, which end contains both the beginning and the middle. So the sense of which we are speaking is essentially dramatic; that is to say, it allows for a breakthrough into higher forms of consciousness. And the outcome, even though its promise favors man's happiness, still allows the widest possible stage for moral choices—and even for lapses.

In this sense, to exist at any given point of time is truly to exist at the end of time. It is to contain and embody in oneself the spiritual resources that will be purified and vindicated at the end. Man is called, by his choices, his moral struggle, to make the end of things present to his life. Tomorrow is possible because of today. Indeed, man lives today as though tomorrow were less than remote. The announced theme of John is "the present, and what will happen hereafter." (1:19) (John was deported, in exile on Patmos; during his stay, he was, as he tells us, granted this vision.)

The vision was essentially that of Christ, Who alone opens his history before the believer. We must recognize in the consciousness of John an immense moral transition; from Jesus, the humiliated servant of God into the understanding of Jesus as triumphant Lord of time. To the believer, He alone opens a credible and coherent vision of man's place in the world.

He is the "first born of many brethren"; that is to say, He is not merely pre-eminent in His biological place. His inmost meaning is that He, being, as John indicates, *Verbum*, offers intelligence and coherence at the heart of things. He is not bound by laws of ancient or modern chaos.

His life and death have been assimilated into the spiritual life of the community. They have long since become a "way," as we note in the Acts of the Apostles. What He offers men is the pre-eminent method or mystique of reaching the Father. It is so simple a thing as the giving of one's life, in faith, for the brethren.

But there is more to be considered. The life and death of Jesus have been accepted by the Father, a unique beginning of what St. Paul names a "new creation." His way is loved by the Father; He is now "raised up."

So a supposition of the Book of Revelation is that Jesus opens history wide. He Himself is that book sealed with seven seals, which He alone is worthy to open. Being both God and man, He is both author and subject of history. As author he unseals the book, when all others are helpless to do so. As subject of history, He is victim, wounded, slain, by that same history. That is to say, He encounters the fact of evil by assuming it in His own flesh. He is the lamb that was both slain and stands again.

In Chapter 6 of the Book of Revelation we are conscious of the symbolism of the "seals." According to the sense of this book, history is commonly sealed before men. Men are unable to reach a viable and workable knowledge of themselves. They are literally unable to imagine themselves in the real world; that is to say, as men having moral weight, and making a difference there. They are seduced by their own rhetoric and the illusions of their ego. And this poverty reaches very deep, to the juncture of bones and spirit. It is not to be relieved by a simple act of the will, or by an improved education. Its relief is quite simply in the ultimate scheme of things, a matter of God's intervention. Only Jesus can open the book.

Nor is the book to be understood as some universal panacea for human ills, an Olympian plan for the whole of history. It looks both outward and inward. In a sense perhaps precious to modern man, "the book" must be understood as a history of consciousness and of choice. Apart from the Lord of history man is unable to reach the choices that grant him life and free him from the powers of death. In this intimate and painful sense, to open the book of history is to open man to himself.

II

It might be worth noting that time in the Book of Revelation is defined as a state of "relation." That is to say, one is truly within time insofar as he is related, in faith and in fact, to Someone. And this Someone is the very hinge upon whom time itself turns. Relationship, friendship, community with Him define events as past, present, and future. He is Himself "the Happening" par excellence. Jesus is the One Who was, Who is, Who comes again. (1, 4; 4, 8) It is only in conscious union with Him that a man may define his own consciousness as passé, truly present and aware, or drawn forward by invitation. Note that the third member of the expression, if it were strictly consistent with the other two, would read rather "He will be." The expression, however, is strengthened enormously by the change in sense introduced by "He comes."

One notes in this regard a further text, almost the closing of the hinge, chapter 22, verse 17, as well as verse 20. "Come Lord Jesus"; or, in the Aramaic, "*Marana tha.*" The "coming again" of the Lord Jesus, as promised, makes a future an assured one, an event, a meeting of persons, defined and understood as the consummation of history itself. There is perhaps no need to dwell here upon the stark contrast offered on the one hand by religious tradition, and on the other by the consciousness of secular man. Jesus offers a personalist vision, utterly gratuitous, an act of God as defining the end of things. Man's highest nobility is vindicated in "choosing to be chosen." But it is God Who, as the Savior so often assisted, chooses to choose. That is to say, the end of things is not a peak of human grandeur or talent—nor is it a stew of degradation and violence. It is an act of God, which is to say, a marriage act, an act of love.

On the other hand, we need not linger long over the obscure, brooding, calamitous sense that nuclear madness has introduced into the consciousness of men today. Man sees the end of things, in his nightmare or his obscene daydreams, as literally the bringing down of creation by a holocaust. In this secular apocalypse, the end of things is a purely human act, an abstract destruction wrought in the image of that sin that Sartre has declared is modern man's particular genius. That is to say, man is now able, as no man before him was able, to render the concrete abstract. The end of things is inevitably annihilation of brothers and enemies alike; simply, the sin which we have come to know by the name "modern war."

"He comes" in our text is echoed in the response of the community in the latter chapters: "Come, come O Lord Jesus." The stress here is upon the authentic freedom of the religious ethos.

Apocalyptic time is a mode of consciousness that includes the present and the future, but always embodied. We are perhaps allowed, in such a case as this, to generalize. Unless our lives include other lives, we are not conscious at all.

It is the property of vision to eradicate distinctions between present and future, and to set forth, in a single moment of ecstasy, the future, precisely *as present*. This would seem to be the meaning of these introductory words of chapter 1, verses 12–16, in which an attempt is made, unique in primitive Christian literature, to describe the Lord.

"I turned round to see who had spoken to me, and when I turned I saw seven golden lamp-stands and, surrounded by them, a figure like a Son of Man, dressed in a long robe tied at the waist with a golden girdle. His head and his hair were white as white wool or as snow, his eyes like a burning flame, his feet like burnished bronze when it has been refined in a furnace, and his voice like the sound of the ocean. In his right hand he was holding seven stars, out of his mouth came a sharp sword, double-edged, and his face was like the sun shining with all its force."

(Note that the term "Lord" is applied, according to a primitive stereotype, only to the risen One.)

Are these words properly a description of Jesus at all? The query is of more than passing interest, in view of the fact that none of the four gospels have ever attempted a physical delineation of Christ. Here, the treatment is entirely symbolic, and the symbols do not sit easily one with another. Our difficulty recurs; the void between language and vision. It is perhaps worth noting once more that the symbols need to be highly intellectualized, in a sense "translated."

Note, the images under which the mysterious One identifies

Himself, chapter 1, verse 17 and following. It is the apocalyptic consciousness in all its grandeur and scope.

An immense spiritual distance is encompassed in the expression, "the First and the Last." There are echoes here of Genesis, Exodus, and Isaiah. This holy One, being conscious, encompasses the beginning and the end of things. He is both creator and consummation. Indeed, a grandiose claim for the despised and executed rabbi!

"The Living One." There are many declarations in favor of life spoken by Jesus in His gospels. One would like to point out here something that I take to be a general truth of all religions. That is to say, if they have anything at all to offer, it is a slight edge of life over death. Authentic religion is the self revelation of a god who, despite all, favors life—who bestows life, loves life, vindicates life, prefers life. One might almost dare to say, likes life. I am at a loss to praise adequately an insight often neglected and despised by those who profess obedience to the God of life. I point with utmost shame and confusion to the war record of Western Christian or post-Christian civilization. One is tempted in hours of despair to conclude that the service of God in the West, has been no more than a millennial service of the gods of death. Christians have not only endorsed organized violence; they have often, during the Crusades and in periods since then, actually consecrated violence as a blessed endeavor, an act of obedience to God.

Everything that follows, in verse 18, is no more than an embolism upon this great title, the Living One. That is to say, the essentially moral and dramatic activity of the Living One is to snatch men from the power of death, and the geography of death, called Hell. Thus life, in its divine form, is revealed to us as an entrance into struggle against the multiple forms of death that afflict men, and presume to claim him for their own.

Death, here and elsewhere, is personified, as is life. Indeed, life in its highest and most transcendent form is simply divine truth, creation, movement, gift.

The more a man's life approaches the divine and draws upon

it (in nobility, moral passion, quality, and style) the more he will enter into the struggle against death. In this regard the dignity of those who surround the throne of the Living One, chapter 4, verse 7, is simply indicated; they are the "living ones." They represent the created universe. And their dignity is that of life itself, which they both receive and convey.

There can be no least doubt about it; Christians are in trouble. Their God is "a living God," so when they abandon Him, it is in favor of what the Old Testament calls simply "the dead"—that is to say, they turn from God to multiple idols, extrapolations of the ego, whether of racism, war-making, hatred, envy, neglect of the poor.

It is the Lamb who alone is capable of opening and unsealing the book. The book is from one point of view human consciousness, and from another, perhaps more literal one, human history. A claim is implicit here that should give thoughtful men pause. Only God, it is implied, can unseal the meaning of being a man, to man himself. Christianity would perhaps add the particular point: Yes, God can do this, but only if He becomes man. So in a sense, man is saved not only in his immortal parts, but in his human pride and dignity. He is saved by a man.

The release of the four horsemen in chapter 6 is sufficiently celebrated. One cannot turn these pages without releasing from them a stench of death. For death is already written upon the pages themselves. It is also written large on the text of every people who claim to be literate at all. That is to say, the invitation that belongs properly to God and is issued by God to man. "Come!"—this invitation is also proper to the powers of death. The power of death always appears as the natural progeny of the power of life. And insofar as possible, they ape the Person of life to the minutest significant detail of word and appearance. We see the same profound insight in the episode of the Beast. One could not, with Auden, "run toward life," without at the same time hearing in one's ears the voice, scarely audible but infinitely seductive, urging man to run toward death.

One points with delight to the little episode in chapter 10

verse 8 and following. The seer is ordered, against all the laws of sound nourishment, to take the book in hand and eat it—literally, to consume it. "It will fill your guts with bitterness, but in your mouth it will have all sweetness of honey." So he did, and so it happened. Simone Weil says that eating is an ocular thing. I think she is saying that when one has truly read, the book gets into his guts. And there it is neither delightful nor suave; it burns and resists passage—perhaps because the truth is literally indigestible to most of us.

Part Two

PROPHETS AND PRISONERS

One

JEREMIAH:
THE WORST IS NOT YET

One is justified in asking at the outset whether Jeremiah appears as a type (in the strictest sense) of modern man in search of a soul. In the case of one ancient man, this search brought him into inevitable conflict with the Powers. It brought him to prison. All of which is not a unique fact in the history of conscience. If Jeremiah has relevance for us, it is perhaps in the intrusive abruptness with which his fiery temperament codes and decodes the heart's message for others. And in the way a man carries, quite literally, his people's sins along with him, as he attempts to live the life of man in public.

A more profound question arises for the desacralized men and women of today. Divine vocation, divine interference in the human scene, instructions from on high; what can these mean in a world of men and women who do battle, live the life of the mind, make love and order their affairs, well or badly, all under the overarching hypothesis that God does not exist? Or if indeed He does exist, that His absence is no more frightful than His presence, and His presence hardly less interesting than His absence?

Another difficulty surely is the strong, even arrogant assumption of "vocation" on the part of the prophet. From his earliest days, Jeremiah turns like a heliotrope in the direction of the Divine. More than that, his being is so infused with, so highly charged with the presence of God, that he is borne backward in time, to the realization that he is indeed a predestined one, from before his birth.

We do well not to deny a man his vision, even though we may not share it. The vision of Jeremiah included a terrifying awareness of human evil. In such a man, the sense of God's omnipotence scarcely can have operated as a personal comfort. Indeed, Jeremiah knew his Gethsemane. Passage after passage have been compared to the Confessions of St. Augustine (11, 18–12, 6, 15, 10–21, 20, 7–18). Always to lie under threat, always to fail, to be the butt of persecution, never to know the sweetness of family or home, all this suffering lay like a stigma upon his sensitive and gentle spirit. Chapter 15, 10–11, 15–21 is a paroxysm of sorrow; it is at the same time a mysterious point of renewal for his vocation. God calls him once more to surpassing moral effort and to progress in the spirit. Suffering has opened his heart to God, and his exchange with the Divine One goes forward in the spirit of the "poor of Yahweh."

Jeremiah was also thrown into prison. It was one ingredient in his long lifetime of anguish. Indeed, such a man could not, given his overwhelming sense of vocation, have hoped to escape the disfavor of public powers. For Jeremiah came from a long line of jealous and God-intoxicated men. Foreign domination was no strange event in their history; what would have been strange, indeed utterly unbearable and unprecedented, would be the abandonment by God of His people. Indeed, as the foreign armies marched upon sacred soil, defiling the temple and the holy places, the enemies merely forced under a greater pressure, into a more incandescent brightness, that flame of holy zeal and holy hatred that was the prophetic gift.

For it does not do justice to the truth merely to note that Jeremiah has a strong sense of vocation. The truth is more concrete and rude; he is formed as a kind of sacred vessel in the hands of a sacred nation. He is fashioned in the image of election, which is his people.

And this is why his life lies under jeopardy—indeed, under double jeopardy. For the times do not favor the development of a holy people. Indeed, they favor and entice away from the right path all those who prefer their well-being to the will of God. So the first conflict within the heart of the prophet, and the first revenge likely to be taken against him, arises from those who worship false gods, who enter into corrupt political alliance, who cast aside moral conduct, who compromise, either materially or formally, the tradition of Israel. (It ought to be a source of comfort, even though indeed of cold comfort, that at certain low points of his public life, Jeremiah issued a medical bulletin, calling his people simply incurable.)

A man profoundly in touch with his tradition, a man profoundly at odds with his tradition. Within these seeming incompatibilities of spirit, the great spirit of Jeremiah moved—and still moves. Which is to say, he sets up resonances and general lines of force, still operative within the spirit of man. Is it possible indeed to live, when such profound moral chasms are opened in one's own spirit by the times one lives in? Or is it not simply a fact that such a man could have lived in no other way; that indeed he was fashioned exactly for such times and *by* such times? There are men who run ineluctably to ruin, for whom the specter of "normal times" is indeed a horror. Times of violent change, of almost universal infamy, the falling away of the faithful from the true way—these awaken the counterpoint of the human spirit to its greatest grandeur.

But we must not see Jeremiah entirely in one light; his spirit evades a single line of analysis. His oracles at times contain elements of profound optimism. Salvation (that tortured and complex notion) is still possible under the hypothesis that the people will expiate their sin. A hundred years of exile, the sufferings of captivity, the siege of the city—all of these help bring about the rebuilding of Jerusalem, the restoration of a Davidic form of rule.

Hints of universal expiation? A vision, a drama of guilt worked out in public and in secret? Jeremiah indeed opens a strange world before most of us. Is it possible that such a vision has meaning for us? A generation that has known an overwhelming measure of wanton destruction and willful evil does not come easily to a personal God Who judges, a rationalism that underpins and ultimately is the ground of things, despite the devouring phenomena of absurdity.

There is a meaning to things, however dark and damaging to man. Jeremiah wrestles with the meaning; his wrestling *is* the meaning; it defines the moral substance and limits of his activity in the world.

At the same time, his struggle with the unknown One interiorizes, draws to a fine point of force and gravity his moral life. Jeremiah, as he comes to understand his struggle, also comes to understand his own heart. And there he sees the Divine Will. One of his finest oracles, praised by believers and unbelievers alike, is the announcement of a New Alliance (31, 31–34). It is of all literature one of the highest expressions of the spirit of man. It outlines a kind of modest Utopia, that moment of the heart and of the community, when men discover God within themselves, when the imminent One stands recognized as the transcendent One.

All of this, and whatever comfort it holds, contained no comfort for Jeremiah. Of his own lifetime, he harvested only personal ruin and sorrow. His influence—indeed, the exalted regard in which future generations have held him—was attained at the expense of his own life and death. But in the nineteenth century, Renan could say unequivocally: "Without this extraordinary man the religious history of humanity would have taken another course."

Christians have paid him their highest tribute. He stands as a limpid and unique type of Christ Himself, preparing within Judaism a new alliance, in person and in freedom. Renan concludes: "Without this man there would have been no Christianity."

It was in a time of imminent doom that God first encountered the prophet. And with a sign (1, 5). A sign that contained within itself its own validity. Like all true signs, it scorns proof. "But I knew you before your birth." It is enough.

Jeremiah was the opposite of a willful Olympian; he speaks in accents of halting deprecation. "I am only a child, I do not know how to speak."

But he is forbidden to trouble himself or waste good time on excuses; before the call of God, they are trivial and irrelevant. The fact is that he is "sent," he is a man "under orders." In the world, God and he form a single, indivisible moral force. It is literally true that God's words are in his mouth. Or better still, the human word and the Divine are one reality, uttering in time a single word of salvation.

The word has to do with principalities and powers. "To pluck up and break down, to destroy and overthrow, to build and to plant." Such a word sounds strangely "destructive" to modern ears. But the word spoken to Jeremiah is an enemy to all gradualism, all theories of history based upon the escalation of goodness. No, God implies, there are times so evil that the first and indeed the only genuinely prophetic function is to cast down the images of injustice and death that claim man as victim. Such are the times in which the prophet has been ordered to speak. It was not a time to build, to improve, to ameliorate conditions that were, to some degree, out of line with the main effort of human goodness. No, the times were judged by God; evil beyond cure. Only a new beginning would suffice.

Of course, a question will always occur as to the difficult analogic content of a passage such as this. Are the present times indeed so evil as to demand a literal reading of a text such as this? It is a question fit to harass the best and purest of spirits. Is the captivation of man by injustice and sin so nearly total as to demand, as a genuine prophetic function, that one first of all "pluck up and break down"?

We are so used to an acculturated and childish religion, whose ethos has joined forces with the society—with its militarism and racism and fear of life, that we are almost illiterate before a document such as Jeremiah's. Can it be true that God is not a Niagara of pablum, spilling His childish comfort upon the morally and humanly neutral, whose faces are raised blankly to partake of that infantile nourishment?

"Therefore I will contend with you." It is at once the highest compliment of God and a guaranty of the dramatic and abrasive quality of life. "And with your children's children I will contend." Every "religious" person would like to see these words addressed to someone other than himself. The parents who are church-goers would like to see them addressed to their sons and daughters who are Sunday renegades. Those in full possession of American power—that is to say, the power of making war and of defrauding the poor—and who help form the articulated backbone of the church in the world would like to see such words applied to the cultural and religious dropouts whose presence offends our decent and sterile horizon. But the Book of Jeremiah offers no such easy out. Indeed, we are granted there the vision of a people who may well be our ancestors—ourselves, wrapped in the robes of self-confidence and of assurance before God. And it is exactly these people who have "defiled, who have gone after the Baals."

No, we must enter a more modest and humiliated landscape of the spirit if we wish to understand Jeremiah.

Two

PAUL IN CHAINS

Whatever the personal convictions of the man who hears handcuffs close upon him, it is clear that society has other definitions than his of human life and conduct. In the cases of both Jeremiah and Paul, the reasons that brought them into public infamy and prison had something to do with a certain disputed definition of the sacred. A definition, translated and embodied in moral conduct, was at variance with public mores. Each of these two men claimed to be in living contact with transcendent mystery. And the mystery was embodied—that is to say, it demanded a visible ethical gesture. But the gesture was forbidden by civil power; at the other end of exalted vision and its style, stern eyes were alert. For good, rational, superficially persuasive reasons, taboos of law-and-order prevailed. Reasons of survival, most of all; the first requirement of the state, which reasons are translated as good order, conquest, the segregation of men according to victim and executioner, and so on.

In a sense therefore it begs the question, and limits the question, to invoke martyrdom in a purely aesthetic or religious sense, as an explanation for the cruelty and suffering imposed upon men of belief on the part of society. A martyr does not suffer or die in a social vacuum; moreover, only in the case of two conflicting religious beliefs does he suffer for anything that might remotely be called sacred reasons. It is not the hammering out of dogma that normally reverberates in the wounded flesh of the suffering believer. And even religious communities somewhere in the depths beyond their rhetoric and suppositions usually inflict suffering on their opposite numbers for reasons that are distressingly prosaic and secular.

This reflection is to the point in regard to Paul, as it was in regard to the more obscure case of Jeremiah. We have no direct or detailed knowledge of the reasons governing the imprisonment of Paul. But we have good reason to believe that he had become a source of discomfort to the forces of law and order. He had not kept his religion in its place, he had not played a good civic nigger. His faith was a source of disruption, in one way or another, in an imperialist state that demanded a wooden-legged and wooden-minded conformity to orders. The case, one dares to think, was quite as simple as that. Paul might indeed be granted the right to worship a dead man, inexplicably risen from the dead; to worship Him indefinitely, and without serious interference. But there was something more; he refused to worship in cellars, or to keep under a bushel the light that had been struck in his mind.

He was in fact asserting once more, at a cultural dead end, the vitality and newness of a message that placed man under public scrutiny, and, inevitably, given the times, under legal jeopardy.

Sacred reasons in the heart; secular reasons in the public domain. The two, each being disposed toward a kind of native fidelity to its own vision of life, cannot be conceived apart from conflict. History shows that the conflict is joined, inevitably. I presuppose here the vitality of both orders of competence. That is to say, it is a function of the secular society, in proportion as its aims become more and more "imperialized," to declare itself sacred. It makes total those demands upon the person which in more normal times might be conceived of as both modest and minimal. In the supposition, however, that the society is enlarging its spheres of influence to the point where man himself is the object of conquest, we have a kind of bastard sacralizing of civic demands. Encroachment and seizure proceed at every level. Criteria for good citizenship are multiplied at every stage of life, indeed, at every street corner. One must constantly prove himself. The proof of the man is not taken in any classic or intellectual or creative measure; it is a simple matter of giving over head and heart to the merchandizing, packaging, and disposal of the imperialist state.

The consequence to the individual, and to the tenor and moral capacity of the society, indeed bear weighing. Man, in this case totally secularized by state order, is at the same time permeated with a kind of idolatrous sacred content. One has only to think of the bestial fervor, the incandescent waves of murderous common intent, that join a lynch mob with the mobs of ancient Rome.

The Bible had a word for it. No longer worshiping or believing man, but man the idolator. And the visage that broods down upon his worshiping form is the visage of immediate, tactile, quantitative, and provable power. One wins in this world; it is as simple as that. One had best, at the expense of whatever spiritual aspiration or act of faith in the beyond or the future or the mystery, lay his cards on this table and place his stake in this world.

It is exactly this project that Paul refused, as a project interpreting his vision of life. The letter to Philemon is instructive in this regard. It is a letter sent from a jail cell to a church gathered, as the letter indicates, in someone's home. The subject under discussion is one of urgent compassion. It is the fate of a runaway slave. Complicated doctrinal or ethical questions do not occur. We have a precious glimpse into the singleness of mind available to a man, when a man undergoes trouble for the right reasons. The complexities of living in the world as though one belonged there, and was not to be seduced or suffocated by the world— these questions of large import, dwelt upon, pondered, wrongly and rightly acted upon through so many centuries, are in a sense swept aside, in order that a single question might be isolated and its import revealed.

The letter is unique, if only for the reason that in it a prisoner is mindful of a slave. A man has detached himself from his own fate, and pleads for a man whose worth to society is calculated at nearly zero. A prisoner pleads for a slave. The public import of religion could not be more simply put or more radiantly indicated.

What drives men to such lengths also exalts them to great heights. That is to say, the most humiliating events enlarge a man's capacity to understand and vindicate the worth of life. The poor go for comfort to the poor, as Peguy has it.

It is good for both believers and humanists to reflect on these things. It is no accident that the believer in jail often looks upon his condition as abnormal (which from many points of view it is) and envisions, in more or less questionable fashion, a return to normal life. He dreams of returning to normal religion, that is, to the agglomerate of observance, property, and mystifying rhetoric that governs most religious groupings and makes them good allies of the state. Cicero puts it in a sentence: "When the priest and senator pass in the streets, they wink at one another."

No wink of the eye was ever exchanged between Caesar and Paul. And in a recent courtroom appearance, David Miller's response to the judge who had just sentenced him was, "Caesar will never have me." He too is in jail. The times have a way, if the times are good enough or bad enough, of forcing an issue, of forcing men back to their roots. And when this occurs, a great measure of the complexity that arises in "normal" life tend to merge, in a few main directions, the movement of the few arteries that support the common life. The believer in jail, mindful of the runaway slave, finds himself drawn strongly toward the brother in the next cell, who is also mindful of the runaway slave. So both become men by living as St. Exupery once recommended: "By looking not at each other, but in the same direction."

The prisoner cannot run; the slave is a runaway. But the slave is a slave, while the prisoner may be a free man. That is to say, the fate of a prisoner, in a world governed by moral slavery, may be preferable; at least for a time, at least to get new symbolism into motion.

But how did the prisoner regard the slavery from which his friend was fleeing? The question has always been a source of rancor between Paul and the revolutionary and secularized community. Was the attitude of Paul toward the slave indeed humane and courageous? Or did he undercut the question of the legal and political reality, using these only as symbols of the slavery of unregenerate man? One commentator puts the matter in this way; you may judge if he is a special pleader: "Paul respected the social condition of his times. He did not aim at abolishing slavery but at humanizing it. He asked that the Christian slave be henceforth treated as a brother; and this was indeed a new idea in a world where the slave was regarded as a mere thing—without a soul, with no rights. Moreover, Paul goes still further and allows it to be understood that he himself expects Philemon to free Onesimus."

We are perhaps less inclined to deal critically with a man who is in prison for reasons worthy of man. At the same time we are justified in questioning narrowly a man whose vision is responsible for a tradition as influential and dangerous as that of Christianity. Might not a revolutionary denunciation of slavery have prevented those later compromises between Christianity and the same institution? We are blind, the best of us, in the midst of conflict, toward the opportunities the conflict itself offers. Moreover, most of our sins, as those sins are raked over in the debris of history, are revealed for what they are; sins of omission. They reflect incomplete areas of our existence that we have not willed into being—fewer limbs than necessary, blind areas of the brain, too small a heart for too large an organism. We have sinned because we have omitted becoming men, the full measure of a man being dictated, not by one's will to become superman, but by the cry of the world that a man inhabit the world as its conscious apex.

There are ways and ways of liberating men. But the only way worth talking about is the way that invites man to liberate him-

self. And the least one may ask of a religious tradition is that it
not dehumanize man in the process of Christianizing him. Religion must not attempt to persuade a man, for whatever sacred
reasons, to resign his normal freedom, his inalienable rights.
We do not admit a colonizing faith; we have had enough of that.

At the same time, the implication of Paul is clear. One must
not conclude that because a man's civil or human rights are
vindicated, he is thereby a free man. The tendency of history,
especially of Western history, is to liberate man in certain precious
and public areas, at the same time progressively enslaving him
in more mysterious ways. And this too must be faced by young
people of the left, the depth and worth of whose moral passion
is beyond question.

That is to say, from a simple, pragmatic point of view, man
is forever enlarging the possibilities of his enslavement, even as
he opens before himself the possibilities of his freedom. Liberation
must therefore continue on those several fronts that the revolution itself has revealed to be fronts of human experience and the
unknown. The revolution is a matter as much of Freud as it is a
matter of Che; a matter of Sakarov as it is a matter of Don
Juan; a matter of Lenny Bruce as it is a matter of Sisyphus.

A few reflections, to conclude.

1. Are not the prisoner and the astronaut two interesting American symbols today? The question, as put, is very nearly unan-
swerable, and to that extent meaningless. What is really of point
is the contention that American outer-space exploration, with the
book of Genesis resounding throughout the universe, is an activity
that approaches the blasphemous. It is relieved of malice only
by the unrelieved and very nearly incurable innocence of those
who take part in such paraliturgy. For the fact is that outer
space itself, and the innovative scientific activity of the great
powers there, is almost totally claimed by the military. In comparison with all this, the immobility of the man in jail, whose
mind is supple before experience, is highly preferable. For at
least it can be said of such a man that he is offered a measure

of space and of purity within which to imagine a form of life worthy of the human.

2. Dislocation, alienation; all the bogey words apply today, with a vengeance. Thereby taboos are applied that make even good men step backward in haste. The point is, of course, that in modern life most valuable people are dislocated and alienated. But the point of dislocation is a new location; that is to say, in a radical sense, a new place to put down roots. And by hypothesis, a good soil is better than a universal macadam parking lot. And as for alienation, a nineteenth-century poet has reminded us of the classical case. It was a biblical girl named Ruth. She was alienated, as he explains, because she found herself amid corn.

3. The brunt of any wave of human change is borne by those whose capacity for sacrifice is quite large. The statement, of course, is complex and needs modifying. Also to be brought into play are resources of imagination, inventiveness, and psychic balance. But we may take it at the same time as apothegm that those who are willing to sacrifice nothing or very little, offer nothing or very little to history. It must also be said that they offer little or nothing to their own soul.

4. To the suffering guru, absolutism is a real and present danger. In Paul's case, the absolute centered around the supremacy of the "Lord." By His sacrificial life and death, and His rising from the dead, Jesus has become bearer of the meaning of the universe. It is from prison that Paul insists, as though from a native rock upon which he stands and will stand, that this Divine One cannot be bought off by all the vain and vainglorious forms of power that the ancient world paid tribute to.

Now such a claim, exercised with such fervor, such indifference to life and death, can represent either a mortal danger or a transcendent opportunity. Follow this one, follow that one. Has Paul merely taken a stand, choosing among all those false and seductive lords of the world who promised salvation in the name of this or that human impulse, extrapolated, personalized, and made absolute as a god?

When men seek relief from some form of slavery, their relief normally takes the shape of a new kind of slavery. I do believe that Paul's case represents a breakthrough. He was not sprung from a prison into a mere prison yard. The door that was opened for him may still yield before the password.

Three

BONHOEFFER:
GOD IS NEITHER HERE NOR THERE

While I was sitting in my apartment, minding my own business, toward midnight on March 17, innocent as the unborn, I had a phone call.

The circumstance is as pathetic as a story by John O'Hara or as fierce and sudden as a tragedy by Aeschylus, the times being what they are. A young Cornell resister announces that his trial for refusal of draft would be held in Connecticut at ten o'clock on the day following. We conversed. In trying to learn the particulars, I felt growing around me the urge that sent Jack upward on the beanstalk, or the Greek into the labyrinth. Elevation, creation, destruction; the old game once more. I went. We spent some six hours in a crowded car, crossing three state borders, into the Sovereign Commonwealth, one more trial of one more resister.

The same? The difference was made manifest in many ways during the hours that followed. Every such trial is a new kind of test case; not the old tired rigmarole of power that disposes of ineffectual or irrelevant men in Kafka or Dickens. Here was the case; a youth who was placing his life, square or round, into the wounds of the world, square or round. A surgical precision. The right action at the right moment.

What was wrong was also usual. That is to say, as in the case of Boston or of Catonsville, an aged judge presiding over the senility of the nation. And in that measure, in that geography, in that courtroom, the judge was unable from the point of view of existence itself to connect with the youth of the nation, the youth of conscience, the passion and goodness that might even spell our salvation. But not yet.

Gary had been up all night. He had worked until 2 A.M. at the Glad Day Press in Ithaca; he then picked me up, and we departed in a Rambler crowded to the gunwales with an unlikely crew. Seven of us, bound for six hours on the road together; predawn, dawn, and the bleak new day that offered nothing new to us. Another day in the long night of resistance.

The decor of the court was both new and old; you could always take your choice where plastic was concerned. ("Think plastic," as the old man advised the young nonhero in *The Graduate*. That is to say, where plastic thinking is concerned, old age or youth are irrelevant. Buy and sell, sellout, profit, this night your soul will be demanded.)

The judge, in the way of plastic, was neither old nor young. It mattered not at all that he was old. He was young in the latest cliché, the latest unfathomable, shallow jargon about who we were, why we were where we were. He was old as the judge of Socrates or of Jesus; he was as young as the judge conducting the Presidio trials. In that sense, one did him an injustice by dismissing him as an old man, sending off a young man to do penance for not dying and killing in the name of Holy State. In a deeper measure, he was simply a witness to the perennial meaning of original sin. He was proving something. He was proving that sin is as old as Cain, and as young as the latest fresh bullet to leave the hot American rifle, to enter the torn flesh of the latest anonymous victim, turning full into the gunsight, dumb and doomed as an animal. He was as old and as young as sin. He was once more proving sin original, in the sense both of its age and its youthfulness. He was old as the myth of Genesis, he was young as the latest lie from the White House. His life had grown old; he had made all things, including death, new.

I enter into all of this in order to enter once more into

the question of Bonhoeffer. That is to say, I do not believe one can, without risk, pick up the prison letters of this man. Can one without risk pick up the New York *Times?* We are being struck in the face by the news that refuses to become new. All efforts to transform our lives into good news for others are constantly being assaulted and battered by the latest bad news, concocted and dumped upon us by the authority of church and state. The good news that we wish to create by our lives is narrowed to that small arc that lies, incandescent and living, between our reading of Bonhoeffer and our sweating in court-rooms.

We are trying to be modest in all respects. We are trying to be modest about our experience, which we believe is nearly the only useful modesty. Therefore, we draw analogies. (We have no heart for proofs, bending our mind to make them or to yield to them.) We do not believe that the case of Bonhoeffer is the case of Comstock. But we are drawn forward by the conviction that history does not confront us in a new mask, in a total darkness. Rather, it shows a face that is partly familiar and partly strange. It partially unmasks, it emerges from our lives, to teach us that no man is totally stranger or totally brother; that no experience of man is totally strange or totally familiar.

Thus the analogic character of things places upon us the responsibility of recognition. We are obliged to admit that certain events occurring in another culture, another political climate, are recognizable by elements common to ours. War-making, racism, nationalism are doctrines consecrated by the state and blessed by the church; they operate abroad and at home with very nearly unlimited sway. Only a small and powerless remnant stands firm. It is made up generally of people discredited in advance by a powerful, totalizing rhetoric of leadership. So the common life of good men is shaken; the unity that joins worship to work, to recreation, to education, to love, is broken.

And in an equally profound sense, the center of attention is dislocated. Men are no longer allowed the luxury of normal times, concentration upon those areas of life that are normally considered as values beyond question: the well-being of the children and of the aged. A cycle is broken. Attention is drawn to resistance, to courtrooms, to jails, precisely because the best youth are being hauled in for illegal resistance. Men find, night and day, that their attention can no longer hearken to the moral passions of good men, and still lie within the beaten track. Religious men are becoming something more than religious; they are becoming men.

Gary was summoned to a Connecticut court. A young man decided to surpass the vocation set for him by the powers of the state, acceded to by the powers of the church. He decided to become neither a statesman nor a churchman. He is going to become a man. And since he is born in a period where it is forbidden to become a man, he refuses also to belong to the state as properly understood or to the church as properly acceded to.

He stands before the judge who acts in the name of the state. His life has rendered other men fortunate; so Gary stands with friends who stand neither with state nor church. He stands also with a priest who has dared the powers both of state and of church, and therefore is worthy to be called, in this supreme hour of the passion of youth, a friend. And that is where I stood, out of seminars, out of honors, out of my past, a hand withdrawn from its glove, a child from the womb, out of all the definitions of a man into which I had been born.

I recall having thought, "What a familiar scene!"

The judge was nervy and hostile. Although almost any statement, in principle, is acceptable before sentencing, he chose to interrupt querulously at every point. Almost as though he could not bear not being totally right, totally acceded to, totally His Honor, at an hour when all such things are most naturally called in question. Gary had ridden with us in the crowded yellow submarine all through that rainy night. He said that he did not want the Cornell community to come to his trial, because so many issues were coming to head on campus, grievous and neglected questions, questions that were even now beginning to exact the revenge of neglected history.

The court was therefore a scene that included many of those back home; longing to be here, and yet obediently there. Almost as though a community had decided to try the strength of its own convictions across the miles, rather than being comfortingly huddled into one place, however comfortless. For the court, as Gary and his friends realized, could no longer be the only place where the future was being forged, at firsthand, out of its raw matter. The times demanded that a few go into court; they demanded at the same time that more compose, set type, get the printed word out, that would tell about institutionalized poverty surrounding the university, the university complicity in that poverty, would continue the task of translating racism into its icy and fiery components: indifference, misplaced passion, fear, dread of change.

The judge cut in, again and again, like a dull, serrated cleaver, never quite excising, never quite healing. The dull surgeon, armed with a dull knife, the extension of dullness of mind and heart. The hack, hacking away at the body of man, making cuts from whole beef, from whole man, indifferently. As Mailer would say, the stockyards of Chicago are the setting. For whatever courtroom, for whatever assembly of men in power, dealing with the powerless.

Gary was cool as fresh ice, or as soul on ice. He pointed out his unwillingness to kill, as so many men have pointed out before. He added, as perhaps not so many have added, that he was unwilling also to fill out forms that would grant him an immunity of sorts. He said that as an educated favorite son of the middle class, he was expected to do best what the middle class always does best—save itself. He pointed out, as few have done, I take it, that the poor who cannot fill out forms and justify their conscientious niceties, go off to die in the crude tradition of those who can manage things in no better way. Gary said that he wished to put before his fellow citizens questions relating to human life. He admitted that the questions he was trying to raise were quite complicated, and could only be settled if many good men would make evident their preference for life over death. Such questions could only be resolved because friends were conversing one with another, and coming to the practical conclusions that their vision of life demanded of them. And he insisted with a kind of laconic modesty, as a man whose talents were elsewhere (he is an artist, and speech is not his strong point) that he would continue to maintain his views in spite of all penalties.

The defense was, as usual, a limping one. That is to say, a defense imposed on a lucid, immediate statement of life tends to approve of things it should never even touch. Let life alone. Lawyers are always second best to heroes. As the Milwaukee Fourteen realized, heroes do not stand in need of lawyers; they stand only in need of discipline and faith. And that is their own responsibility, realized in the measure of their own talents, not in the measure of imported or airlifted skills.

Gary's lawyer, a new man on an unfamiliar scene, insisted upon something that, after the statement of the defendant, one could only find pathetic: Such a man as this is not "rehabilitated" through a jail sentence, he declared. What need of affirming things already so well known to all except the blind or the unconscious?

I will refer here to my scribbled notes. The judge riposted that he was still lingering around the "solution" of jail as a protection of society. It was a cat-and-mouse game. He pointed out that the defendant now had a criminal record; his future as a normal citizen was in jeopardy. But, he continued, this record could possibly be erased by the indulgence of the courts, by invoking the Youth Correction Act. Submitting to a sentence of two to six years, Gary could be declared rehabilitated by the parole board and so returned to normal American life. That is to say, he could eventually enter any of the desirable professions, from certified public accountant to mortician. Enough said.

The government was invited to respond to this. The invitation was accepted with a lunge of alacrity. The prosecutor seized upon the dangling alternatives held before the court. He objected in civilized fashion to the possibility of a suspended sentence, to be spent working in a hospital, subject to the scrutiny of a parole board. He appealed to tradition. And to those without a tradition, his appeal had a certain plausible charm. Equal fate for all, the argument ran; why let this one off, when others serve, or are sent to jail? The argument, crude and seductive as the times, invades the courtroom, forbids any deviation by those who stand there, naked and unrecognized, in the very form of the ragamuffin refugees who once set in motion the American experience.

The judge was neither eloquent nor, indeed, audible. (Either contingency was beyond realistic hope; we were humbled by our experience of courtrooms.) He muttered something to the effect that a diversity was apparent across the country, and that judges seemed more disposed these days to grant suspended sentences than heretofore.

The government rejoined, fitting the argument as neatly as one iron gear fits another; yes, but the quality of *sentences* seems everywhere to be the same.

Still, said His Honor, in the case before us, this young man will bear the burden of a criminal record if he is granted a suspended sentence. So there will be some earmark (the word is literally his; something to do with runaway slaves) of deterrence (a word used in other contexts—but perhaps still in the same context) for others; though it must be admitted that the defendant is not to be considered a threat to society.

Then came one of those rare admissions indulged in by almost every judge in whose court we have sat, during the long, recent years of the American experiment in disposing of political deviants. His Honor admitted that there was merit in the case of the defendant. It was as though, with a limb caught in a trap, a man still ventured to speak, as a free man, of what lay outside the trap. Or perhaps he was dealing in the fiction that he was not trapped at all. In any case, after a brief sojourn in freedom, undertaken for the sake of the public media, or of the various sweating friends of the defendant (or in the case of certain favored trials, the presence of newsmen and of marchers in the streets outside), His Honor once more accepts his fate; a captive limb, the steel teeth that had closed upon it. The bite was on.

The judge, after admitting the troublesome nature of the questions facing the young, returned to the facts; deviation, penalties, and jail. He opened his book. The sentence was pronounced.

For a neophyte, it was a puzzling scene. The newsmen poised their pencils, the stenographer's eyes glassed over, the sentence droned on. Such and such section of such and such law. Was the judge speaking of service in hospitals, of a law pertaining to correction of youth? On and on. Finally, the terrible words were pronounced. "Therefore, the defendant is sentenced to from one to six years in accord with the Youth Correction Act." Amen.

In the mad March days, every human folly becomes possible. It is possible to draw the noose tighter on the history of free acts, on lucid, factious youth. From Bonhoeffer to Comstock. As the years turn, and cultural differences become both more apparent and of less import, other men arrange the knot in the rope, pronounce the sentence, announce the horror and folly attendant upon a new effort to justify death.

The final twist is this: Such activity has less to do with the fate of the condemned than with the fate of the hangman. On such a conundrum we may leave the fate of Gary, and enter more deeply into the fate of Dietrich.

The document called "After Ten Years," included in *The Prison Letters*, can by no means be taken as a final testament. Still, it is of capital import in Bonhoeffer's thought, if only because in its pages he planted a seed that came to flowering in his last letters. Many of the ethical and moral considerations that he had pondered for years in jail are summarized here. The manner is laconic and seminal, and leaves almost endless room for speculation as to what his later development might have been. And this veiled genius of his, cut short by death, is surely part of the charm, the obscure almost vatic import of his reflections.

We may reflect at some length on the so-called "six solutions," that he finds in every case inadequate, even though largely operative, in times of crisis.

1. He speaks, first of all, of the failure of *reasonable* people. Such words immediately strike resonance. Indeed, his discussion seems uncannily directed toward our own times, if only because our times are marked by a darkness so like his own. The failure of reasonable people is a constant failure; it is the failure of power in the breach. On the American scene, it has to do most recently with the decline and fall of those liberals who once placed their stake in the Kennedy spirit and method. When that spirit was violently withdrawn, they drifted from McCarthy or Humphrey through the meager, desperate effects of recent political charade, into a nest in the White House. They tried, those reasonable people (declared Bonhoeffer) to do justice to all sides; so the conflicting forces wore them down, with nothing achieved. Exactly. It is the failure of people who have neither the courage or insight to diagnose the ills of life deeply enough to admit profound change to their own lives. Their grasping at straws is the outward aspect of their inward disarray in face of the demands of life. They go down before the storm, like liberals before reality. They disappear into a scene, no matter how chaotic or evil, with nothing to offer it except a salve, a Band-Aid, a blessing—it is all the same: cowardice, legitimacy offered to the evil times they could not resist. Meantime, simply something like this is left to us; 1969 is the year of obsequies for the unreconstructed liberal, whether political or religious. Send him a wreath. May he rest in peace.

2. The *fanatic* comes under scrutiny next. His plight is not merely uninteresting historically; it is pathological. He is ill; the name of his illness is "definitive solution." He has come upon one method for bringing everything to a good end. (It is interesting that the notes on the fanatic were composed by the victim of the supreme fanatic of modern times.) This man had first entertained the notion of a "definitive solution," thereby solving the "problem" of six million lives. Thereby he had

pointed the way toward massive social solutions, using death as instrument and means. And he had offered, despite his own defeat, a constant temptation to other men of power to entertain the same lethal and evil dreams, the attainment of power through the death of others.

It is not to be thought that the temptation to the "one solution" afflicts only those who are in positions of policy. It also afflicts those who are seeking to offer alternatives to the noxious directions of public life. It is a fact that as men grow weary of their tasks, they seize upon one or another alternative as being the only possible alternative. They lose all perspective. They lose the faculty of listening. And so they come to decide that men must bend in their direction, their direction being the only one. In such a way they accept, willy-nilly, the methods of their adversaries. Their moral being disappears.

3. The man of *conscience* is also insufficient to meet the needs of the times. This appears a more surprising statement, in view especially of the conscience of Bonhoeffer himself, and what might be taken, from a superficial reading, as the sufficiency of his conscience to triumph over the power of death. By no means. It is the man of conscience who rejects conscience as a sufficient resource of man.

Undoubtedly Bonhoeffer is speaking of conscience in a restricted sense, the sense which modern man attaches to it: unattached and free, owing tribute to no "other," no transcendence. It is to be noted too that Bonhoeffer has no difficulty with conscience as a resource in normal times. That is to say, the good man is sufficient to a situation that does not include moral crisis. He will make it, as long as he has only to deal with the demands of the tribe, modern man's equivalent to food-getting and house-building. It is when death is in the air as a seductive and universal voice, that conscience is unequal to the task. During such times, men will have to fight almost alone to confront the universal appeal of those who "know better" what is acceptable and what is not. In such circumstance, which is the very fact and fiber of modern life, the man of conscience is torn to pieces. His goods are not good enough. He is searched out and destroyed by marauders, who called themselves in the midst of their murderous action, pacifiers. Such a rhetoric the man of conscience cannot oppose for long. Bonhoeffer says that he will be rendered nervous and vacillating; the consciences of evil men are stronger than his own.

4. The man of *duty* is equally assailed. (It should be understood here that Bonhoeffer is speaking in the German context. The notion of duty is taken as the sum of all those social and political pressures, strongly in the air in his culture, pressing upon man their imperative to move his life in a given direction.) The critique upon duty states simply that duty will never suffice if one is to meet the realities before one. For in such a case, man is commanded to remain in effect unreflective and childish. He cannot grow up to the point where he can say "No." And that is exactly the rub. Because the times around him are murderously adult; and it is only an adult, seeing on his left hand 2, and on his right hand 2, who can say in his mind that $2+2=4$. To proclaim such an elementary truth may, in some circumstances, require his life.

This is, of course, not to deny that legitimate authority, in whatever sector, must not win the respect of a thoughtful man. But this is a far different thing from declaring that authorities are allowed full unexamined control of a man's moral life. Who is to be trusted? It is a large question. It can be taken as a truism in times of crisis that those forms of political authority which create the crisis seek its resolution in one invariable way, adopted to insure their own survival and well-being. That is to say, public power mandates death as its method, and enlists the citizenry to execute the method. A man who stands in his own shoes cannot but be shaken by such a call of duty, reaching even to the marrow of his bones, seizing upon his very life. Will he ask, "To what end?" To do so is simply treasonous; such a question insists that one's own conscience is the arbiter of his destiny.

We were returning from Hanoi, escorting three prisoners of war

back to America. In the ICC plane in Vientiane, the American ambassador turned the screws upon the released airmen, demanding
peremptorily that they depart our company and return home by
military plane. The eldest of the airmen, a Major Overly, responded, "The voice of my commander is the voice of duty. We
shall go." It mattered little to him at that moment, when the
"voice of duty" had been heard, that other voices had also been
heard, and that he had hearkened to them. At that moment he
forgot the fate of his fellow prisoners; he was willing to place their
fate in the breach at a given order. A kind of total amnesia
overtook him. He seemed unable to remember what promises
he had made, what loyalties he had entertained, even a few short
hours before. There was no better example in my lifetime of the
iron sway over men demanded by military duty.

5. Next, the man of *freedom*. Here it seemed to me Bonhoeffer
is less clear. As far as one can judge, he is speaking of the man
who values his freedom highly, and looks upon it as an indispensable tool in opening the truth of the world. But such a
man falls short; his tool is inept or dull. And this, because freedom has led him into the dark area of compromise and
fruitlessness. He wants above all to act, he wants to act well;
but he has no principle on which to draw, and so is found entirely
at the mercy of this or that expedient, his only warning arising
from the danger he wishes above all to avoid, the danger of the
"worse choice."

I found Bonhoeffer's language somewhat obscure, and his treatment of the question somewhat unsatisfactory. It seemed to me
that a discussion on the dangers of freedom might better have
centered around the necessary inclusion of the will to sacrifice,
as an ingredient of the will to be free. That is to say, if one
is looking only to self-aggrandizement as the measure of the
increase in his freedom, he is merely indulging in another form
of selfishness. He will be unable to stand firm in situations that
may well demand the sacrifice of his life as the price of his
survival as a free man. But perhaps this is what Bonhoeffer is
getting at all along.

6. Finally, the man of *private virtuousness* is declared null and void. This is perhaps a more obvious question, especially in view of our experience of the last few years. It is humanly impossible for a man to act alone and still act well.

And this is so true that modern war is the highest expression of private virtue on public display. War today inducts into public service all those private notions of virtuous self-defense, loyalty, and patriotism that demand public ground for their true, most splendid expression. And how mightily those virtues are inflated once they are set to goose-stepping to the blare of fife and drum! What they are offering to private virtue is public duty. One is not in those ranks freely; one is not free not to be there. Indeed, not to be there is a crime against the state, and places one in an equivalent position to the enemy wherever, whoever he is, whose obscure presence joins the ranks into so close a metallic fabric.

But how shall one say "no" to the beckoning of those hands, and say it alone? He simply cannot. The force of communal might in the modern world can be endured only by a man who has found a true alternative to that might, in the spirit. And that demands that one oppose to the heterogeneous and chancy juncture of force, the deliberate, organic joining of nonforce. That is to say, only the community can confront noncommunity, the platoon, the army.

Bonhoeffer thus ends his diagnosis of the men who were good, but not good enough, who very nearly made it but did not make it. It is his diagnosis of the good natural pagan, who strives to surpass both bad paganism and bad Christianity, bad politics and bad militarism. And such a man falls in the breach. One can only surmise what years of experience, what anguished insight into the insufficiency of human means, led Bonhoeffer to this rigorous, almost surgical diagnosis of modern man. It is to be noted too; it is not evil that he is diagnosing; it is the illness that goes by the name of goodness.

It goes by that name, but the reality is something other. The reality is that of an organism unfit for the times, unready, in its present stage of development, for the organisms, armed, toothed, and clawed, that confront the good man; whose purpose, under whatever pretext, is to render real goodness, real men, extinct.

"Who stands fast?" The question could have been asked only by a man who had himself stood firm, who in face of prison and death declared the insufficiency of modern humanism to survive and surpass modern life.

Four

GANDHI:
THIS MAN IS DISARMED AND
DANGEROUS

In the light of everything we have suffered and inflicted since the bones of this little man went up in smoke, the following reflections may be of point:

1. Let us by all means, and in the name of the honored and dishonored dead, discuss the difference between "saving face" and "changing hearts." Or, if you will, the difference between political solutions (which in modern times always go by the name of "definitive solutions") and what the biblical and Eastern traditions call simply "conversion."

2. Could we think about modern man as guerrilla, refugee, displaced person, prisoner of war?

3. An act of faith by modern man might begin by not asking for a clearer situation than the one he is in. I submit that such an act would be practically heroic.

4. Gandhi's spinning wheel, versus the wheel spinning around and within; the city as history.

5. No one dies in the world he was born into; the moral life as a space ship.

6. Immortality belongs to those who want it badly enough. So does extinction.

7. Pacification: taking it out first of all on humanity.

8. Piety toward the natural order. Impiety toward the natural order.

9. Gandhi's life and death are an example of a constant law: Most human beings (but not all) fall far short of humanity. The Bible said the same thing, for a long time. The Jews, probably because they have always had a classic minority stance before the onslaught of the *goyim*, have placed their act of trust in what the prophets call a "saving remnant." That is to say, their hope is simply in their own historic situation, as God has cast some measure of light upon it. It seems better, the times inevitably being what they are, to be the victim rather than the predator. Even from the point of view of survival, it seems better. The incapacity of the victim to survive is unproven. It cannot be adduced simply because he has been chewed up in this or that instance. Indeed, this or that instance may show him how to escape the next time. But the predator who becomes a congenital predator, that is to say, who needs seriously to disturb the balance of nature in order to survive, becomes too big to survive.

10. The Fall of Western Man Today—Colonialism. The Redemption of Western Man Today—Resistance. Can you translate?

11. A few people have brought on imminent world collapse by their decisions, or have inherited the power that has first set collapse into motion. They ought, a certain number of them, to be resigning from the high places from which they either see collapse and say nothing, or enable it to occur. They ought to be saying what they see. But the system in the mind is so seamless an extension of the system in public that power doesn't get around to reflecting on itself to the point of becoming appalled, or courageous.

12. "Symbolic motions" are the nonviolent (so they say) response of the state to the need for real change. Measure, for example, Martin Luther King's death against the Poor People's March, and the outcome of both.

13. Adjustment to lesser evils; the last infirmity of (formerly) flaming liberals. They came in like crepes suzette; they went out in the perfumed guts of the powerful.

14. Most of us can't find unpolluted air, or benevolent police,

or civilized wards, or political authority that speaks in a sane way. We are really left with very little; enclaves of underdeveloped people in an overdeveloped society, huddling in the night. About all we can do is to refuse to be eaten. Hell, no, I won't go. Violence stops here. (Believe it; the noble stain spreads; its first property is to spread!)

15. Some people ponder Ophelia in order to find out who Hamlet is. Listen to those who go mad this year, in this society— they may be telling us how to get driven sane.

16. How about this, in the light of Gandhi? The author is a Spanish priest, Joseph Dalmau, in resistance against Franco: "A pacifist in the image of Martin Luther King must know that if white power is destroyed by violence, a step forward has nevertheless been made. It is true that the law of violence will continue, but this violence is destined to assimilate the blacks and liberate them, to see that the dignity of the black man is done justice not only in word but also in deed. The important thing is to put the omnipresent enemy out of action."

17. Or consider this, by the same priest: "I affirm therefore the primacy of the objective to be reached over the means used to obtain it, violent or nonviolent." How about Gandhi: "The purity of means determines the purity of the end."

18. Or this: "The death of Che, precisely because he used violence, did not arouse a great reaction among the apolitical ignorant peoples, the majority on our planet. The violence of Che was neutralized by the violence of the Bolivian government. Che murdered, and was murdered in turn. No further comment is necessary. He cashed in on the only money he recognized. The assassination of King, on the other hand, aroused the indignation of simple people everywhere."

19. Or this: "Killing Martin Luther King is killing an innocent man. Killing Che is killing an antagonist. To kill the innocent is a grave matter. To kill an antagonist who was ready to kill you is a current happening, an accepted normal event. On this account the death of King caused so much more commotion than the death of Che."

20. Or this: "If violence appears to have accomplished more than nonviolence in recent history, this could be explained by the fact that nonviolence is a new method, while violence comes to us from our distant animal past. The law of the strongest is a law dating from prehistoric times. The law of love, including the love of one's enemy, comes to us from fairly recent history, almost from outside. It draws us nonetheless like a magnet; witness the power of its historic incarnation from Jesus to Gandhi."

21. Or, finally, this: "I do not finally condemn violence. But I consider that the nonviolence of King is the most efficacious method, as well as the most ethical, in the battle for brotherhood and justice. I condemn only those who are neither for one thing or the other, who knowing what is going on, do nothing while they call upon religion, prudence, and common sense."

22. The nonviolent man does not announce that something new is going to happen in the future; he announces that something new is currently happening. Or, better still, he is making it happen.

23. "But society simply cannot be conducted that way, it falls apart." The edge has been taken off that news, by newer news; society has already fallen apart. What keeps the news from all of us is that we have two stakes in its falling apart: (a) We live off its illegitimacies because (b) we've fallen apart ourselves.

(The following questions on China seem of point, given the current American direction of things. The questions were prepared by Neal Hunter, an Australian who lived many years on the Chinese mainland, returning in 1968.)

24. How is China to defend herself? Why does the West see her small standing army and rather amateur militia-guerrilla forces as a threat? Why does China's lack of an air force and navy seem sinister to the Pentagon? What part does fighting play in the lives of individuals? Is everyone taught hate and killing? Why does China not have a bigger and more modern army anyway, surrounded as she is? Is there something about military life that still doesn't sit well among Chinese? Or have the years

of war made everyone as bloodthirsty as Americans? Does China experiment with germ and chemical warfare? What is the point of her H-bomb? With thermo-nuclear weapons in her possession, is China any different from Western countries? Will the bomb not destroy her people's minds, as it has done to the minds of the West?

25. How valid is the charge that China is violent? We think of Mao's overt shockers: "War is the continuation of politics." "Political power comes from the gunbarrel." We think of her built in emphasis on struggle and war between classes. Do such ideas vitiate or enrich the Chinese contribution to world civilization? (The same question, of course, applies to Black Panthers, Angola guerrillas, Camilo Torres, the Viet Cong, and other otherwise nice people. Not to mention the United States Army.)

26. China's culture, like other cultures, has always had a system of admiration ethics. Education by saintly examples. What do Chinese heroes tell us of our own culture? Who are our heroes? Can the Third World learn better from Lei Feng or Steve McQueen?

27. Can the Chinese people survive indefinitely on the spiritual content of modern communism? Or will there be a reversion to overtly religious rituals, liturgies, devotions? (Can Americans survive indefinitely on the spiritual content of nationalism-*cum*-Christianity? At what cost, to whom?)

Five

A CAMUS GLOSSARY

ABSURD

The gap that exists between the actual shape of life and the
definitions given it by the various forces of church, state, education, family, business, professional life. The absurd is compounded
by ambiguity, falsehood, convention, justification, the law, evasions,
everything that infects a struggling civilization with "the plague."
It is a fact that there is air around us, available to our lungs.
It is also a fact that this air is polluted. But it is absurd that
people accept the fact of pollution, and construct air conditioners
to make it bearable, all the while allowing the culture and
technocracy to dump tons of vaporized garbage into the atmosphere. (For suggestions as to the moral equivalent of all
this, consult your local minister, priest, rabbi, or favorite humani-
ties professor.)

Examples: "Why do you call me 'sir,'" said the prison chaplain,
"why don't you call me 'father'?" "You are not my father,"
said the condemned prisoner, "you are with the others." And
the example alluded to in the second letter to a German friend.
The priest-chaplain who draws the attention of the guards to
the escape of a young prisoner, on his way to being executed.
"A second in which the man of God must decide whether he is
on the side of the executioners or on the side of the martyrs
in keeping with his vocation. But he has already knocked on the

partition separating him from his comrades. The alarm is given."
Finally, as example of religious absurdity, the Père Paneloux,
the "compleat Jesuit" of Oran in *The Plague*. He thinks that religion exists in order to "prove something." This has to do, in
his case, with an apologetic for religion that will make of God
the prime inquisitor of all; the great final judge between the
righteous and the outsiders.

COMPREHENSION

The act of including, as in the act of love. Or in the act of
faith. Or in the act of trust. The graceful and gentle outreach
of the mind in the direction of embodied value. The closest
analogy being the graceful and gentle outreach of the arms, in
the same direction, for the same reasons. Tarrou in *The Plague*
builds what we might almost call a monastic ascesis of comprehension. It would seem to be a key idea with Camus. It
demands first of all a constant *attention*. The mind, in order
to include the world, must come to "the still point of the turning
world." Every activist, if he is not to heap chaos upon disorder,
is called to contemplation.

Secondly, the comprehending man is, of necessity, in exile. His
center of gravity is not the pestilence. He does not accept the
corrupt benefits of a corrupt society, all the while proclaiming
a rhetoric of moral superiority. There is a certain continuity between his moral fabric and his speech; he lives at the edge of
whatever establishment, whatever culture, whatever political form
he is trying to converse with, indeed to be a contributing part
of. But he has distinguished, in his own soul, responsibility from
rewards; and while he multiplies the former, as cell added to
organic cell, he progressively casts off the latter, as an accumula-
tion of poison and antigrowth. His spirit can grow only if it refuses the fattening soporifics of the society; its enticements to
"get with it, get real, grow up, join the club." We are speaking
here of the enormously dangerous, exhilarating, and difficult high-
wire act required of the man who has chosen to walk the wire,

rather than to fall to left or right. And yet who knows that to fall to left or right is practically the destiny of all men born. And that it is not the high wire that places him above other men, or the fact that he has survived so far—a feat in any case as much of good luck as of skill. In any case, he is not upon the high wire as a feat of exhibitionism or ego. He is there because there is another side to be reached, and this is the way.

Finally, one may be called, through this process, to become a "saint without God." Such a conception, as it seems to me, is to be translated, not as a form of atheism, but as a reaction against the "reward obsession" of most Christians. To be virtuous without God is to refuse the bribe under the table. It is to reject the childish conception of a childish God, which obliges Him to comfort the infant at the end of the day with an all-night sucker.

I do not mean to deny that the critique of Camus upon the question of God goes much deeper than his response to the immaturity of Christians. He saw, as all of us see, large numbers of traditional believers whose lives do not exceed the moral equivalent of a communal playpen, inhabited by the feckless and the harmless. The deeper question of whether or not he saw in his heart the drama of the death of God, and buried Him out of sight, out of mind, is colored by at least one fact. That is, Camus declared a consistent nonviolence to be impossible without the postulate of the existence of God. In this rigorous judgment, he seemed mysteriously to have joined hands with the spirit of Gandhi, who had often and overtly stated the same convictions; a man could only embrace a lifelong nonviolent position if he was in touch with the living God.

GRACE

Check one: (1) The state of self assurance by which the elect convince themselves of their superiority. (2) Abstract ethical ideas that justify respectable people in pursuing "pacification," "escalation," "wars on poverty," "South African investments," counter-violence to counter the above violence. (3) The itch to do something in order to prove something; or, conversely, the itch to prove that one is someone, because he has done something.

LIFE

One of those "modest" words upon which the existence of Camus pivots, glows, shapes itself. As a consequence of this choice, one is able to perform a single act in two steps. (1) He breaks across his knee the steel yardstick of the meritocracy, as that cold instrument is commonly placed against human flesh and spirit, in deciding about who will live and who will die. (2) One chooses the life of his brother, already present in the mysterious recesses in which one has chosen his own life. And the two choices are a single, seamless act. In fact, it may well be that the first fact of consciousness is the consciousness of one's community, in which he is included (or, Camus would say, "comprehended"). Life, like hair, belongs to the community. It ought not to be cut off without the agreement of the community. Thus it becomes intolerable that some absurd philosophy or "method" or "solution" should decree, at the mad moment of some mad power, that one's brothers throughout the world be killed in war, executed, jailed, exiled, or in some way disgraced and cast out; all of this for defying the accepted death-dealing myths about what a human being is.

Two things, as they say in mathematics, therefore follow. (1) A man must live in revolt against a public philosophy of nihilism and murder. (2) One is required to move to the side of the victims of the absurd and bestial, the behemoth that claims our lives in its jaws. Thus the deepest meaning of the will toward life is the patient building of forms of community. They offer, here and now, an alternative to the death wish, the militaristic wish, constantly played out across the bodies of the fallen, as the mandarins stretch the wishbone of man to the breaking point, and grind his bones to make their bread.

MODESTY

A realistic self-assessment; man cut down to size. The means is that complex web of moral choice, evasion, hope, and agony that add up to a position, a visible locale in the world. To be a man is to be modest. In this sense, man grows down rather than up; it is the world that purifies him of *hubris* as he outgrows his self-esteem, his murderous will to announce himself abstractly and dogmatically as superior to others. The model of all this is Tarrou. The antimodel of all this is the citizenry of Oran. "Our townsfolk were not more to blame than others; they forgot to be modest, that was all, and thought that everything still was possible for them, which presupposed that pestilences were impossible." In a more grandiose age, the word was perhaps humility; it separated the saint from the grandee, secular or sacred. It presupposed a certain graceful and accurate awareness before the universe, before God and one's community. In a sense, it presupposed that there was an ordered universe up there, governed by a God Who Himself was of both heroic and servant stature.

The word of Camus is spoken in a different universe; it carves out its own moral structure and form, the heroic has dissolved before the penetrating light of a secular century. One is now modest in relation to immodesty, just as one was formerly humble in relationship to diabolic or superhuman pride. Formerly a man, responding to the divine, entered into an ordered and coherent universe, whose structure was a "given." It was verifiable in a continuous history, of minds and communities in harmony. It supposed a certain attitude toward an inheritance of the spirit. But with Camus, all this seems to be altered. Man is now required to be personally heroic, in the very denial of his capability of achieving heroism. Surrounded by egoism, violence, and prometheans, a man can survive spiritually only by playing the antihero. He forms his life by refusing the game. He cannot offer coherence against incoherence, much less can he accept bankrupt forms of power. So he is left with a few paltry, precious possessions of the mind and heart. A sense that life is still supportable and worth the gamble for its own sake. A sense that language ought to correspond to the difficulties of coming even one step or two along the road to truth. A sense that whatever coherence is possible in one's soul or in the universe at large must be a laborious construct, assailed at every point; forever, like Sisyphus, a man begins anew.

PROOF

Aus mit! The proof of the pudding is in the eating. That is to say, life is for the sake of life and is not to be subordinated to anything beyond it. One is not to draw his rules for acting in the real world from men already assimilated to a world of mechanisms, of controllable things, dedicated to the assumption that the control of human beings, in the name of whatever god, is the supreme human enterprise. The point of human existence is that it is unprovable. Either it stands free or it falls. Thus to set out to prove that God ought to exist (or, indeed, that He does not exist) is an enterprise as worthy of a human mind as setting out to prove that concentration camps or sweatshops or nuclear installations (or draft boards) also ought to exist. In both cases, a man seeks for an inhuman justification for the fact that some enterprises have grown too much, too hot, too heavy, too uncontrollable, to deal with. The day on which such proofs are sought, or hearkened to, the human enterprise has been debased almost out of recognition. (It is by now estimated that even the next limited war will employ robot soldiers in place of armed men. And this is exactly what we are talking about.)

One way of defining that rarest of phenomena, a human community, is to say simply; it is a group of friends who feel no need, no "connection" with the necessity of proving anything about their lives. (Department of Entomological Curiosities; "Proof, tested or proved strength, as of armor. Fact, documents, etc., that are so certain or convincing as to demonstrate the validity of a conclusion beyond reasonable doubt.") (Webster Abridged Dictionary) Ha! One may feel impelled, as it seems Camus was impelled, to bring to mind the vast and murderous machinery of human conflict, from inquisitional days to the camps of Hitler, in order to illustrate the determination of man to prove himself righteous, civilized, religious, humane, advanced, morally superior, etc. One may then decide for himself, in whatever secret recess of his heart; no matter what the moral pressures of no matter what church or state or agglomeration of accusing eyes, he will in some garden, play Christ rather than Judas. He will prefer to receive the kiss and the treason and death that follow than to inflict them. This, according to one metaphor, seems to place Christ at the side of the historical method of Camus, rather than of—who? Fill in your favorite man of power. He is out busily, as Dean Rusk says, doing mischief in the world. Or perhaps more simply, and from the straight point of view more acceptably, proving something.

REBEL

"I put all my pride in the belief that the splendor of the world also justifies me and all the men of my race, who know that there is an extreme point at which poverty always rejoices in the richness of the world. Being naked always implies physical liberty, harmony between the hand and the flowers it touches, loving understanding between the earth and the men who have been freed from human things. Ah, I could become a convert to this, if it were not already my religion." (Notebooks, page 57.) "If someone told me to write a book on morality, it would have a hundred pages and ninety-nine of them would be blank. On the last page I would write, 'I recognize only one duty, and that is to love.' And as far as everything else is concerned, I say no." (Notebooks, page 54.)

(In what follows, I pay my debt to Thomas Merton, who in the last two years before his death assembled mimeographed notes for a book on Camus, which was cut short by his own death.

I am drawing on his notes, necessarily fragmented and incomplete, for the thoughts that follow. The honorable joustings are Merton's. The windmills are my own.)

Modern revolutions, like all revolutions, start out by affirming liberty; they consummate their efforts in tyranny. Pleading for a more abundant life, they ended under a single sign; hecatombs of political victims. It appears a matter of concern to Camus that revolution, beginning with the accepted and indeed rejoiced-in "death of God," is unable to work out a morality worthy of man. So the Kingdom of God and the realm of grace are very like flowers on the tomb of God. The realm of justice, so the claim goes, is raised on that tomb. But something has gone wrong. The revolution proceeded from declarations of justice, straight as an arrow into a reign of execution and murder; it demanded the complete suspension of liberty. In the whole process, death was honored, in view of a consummation indefinitely postponed. In the name of something called the secular version of the Kingdom of God, every violence, every cruelty became permissible and even logically necessary.

The rebel comes on another way. Somehow, he comes to realize that the rebellion is nullified when it resorts to the same old method of achieving change—massive death. When the revolution begins to require death in order to oil its gears, it is obvious that it is merely the retooling of the old murderous machinery. When the first declarations of "love of life" have turned into a need of the deaths of thousands, then the reasons that set the revolution in gear are contradicted, and absurdity and nihilism are again in command. That is to say, nothing has really changed at all. "Absolute liberty becomes a prison of absolute duty." The "death of God" comes to mean an imperialism of the spirit that seeks world control at the price of unlimited murder and terror. Note, please, that this insane logic is operating in both the East and the West, whatever cultural conditions and economic forms follow upon the acknowledged need of human change. The labor camps of the Soviets or the Red Chinese are inseparable, in fact as in moral comprehension, from the concentration of nuclear devices and improvements of weaponry in the West. The same logical power and terror grows out of radical godlessness that first grew out of misconstrued Christianity. In such a case, the only sane response of a thoughtful man is: A plague on both your houses.

"Thus starting from the absurd, it is not possible to live revolt without reaching at some point or other an experience of love that is still undefined." (Camus, diary.) The question of love and the question of that which is still undefined. We have touched a point that links absurd men of today with any resister of the past; the presumption that a man, armed with belief, could be finished off by the powers of this world, or the powers of any other world. In remaining outside definitions at the same time that he remained in service to man and in opposition to the forces of death, Camus began in his secret life an adventure that both Marxist and Christian unite in calling the creation of the new man.

"You cannot create experience. You must undergo it. We wait patiently—or rather, we are patients." (Diary, May 1935.) Yes, yes.

THIRD

The number, according to Camus' thought, has nothing to do with astrology. It has rather something to do with metallurgy; the metal that makes the man. The "third" is the choice that lies in the middle, between the extremes of Western capitalism and historical Marxism. Camus could no sooner become a Sartrian than he could become an American. So he aligned himself with powerlessness in order to come up with alternatives to the big "man-grab" of existing powers. There was no point in admitting to a stalemate. Nor was there any point in becoming arbiter between winners or losers. The fact was this: whoever might win in such a game, everyone lost. One might better try a different choice; to walk out on the scene. Such a copout might be the only way of getting in; given the premise that the only "in scene" worth struggling for was a real world, where the only available choices were between forms of death; between the talons of the eagle and the arms of the bear.

The third option, I submit, is the only one worth exploring by rational men. It is one that passionately engages everybody who is conscious of the visual insults of the public media, or who has felt in his face the rotting stench that breathes from the daily papers. But whence shall good news come, except from good men?

The first and second parties have given up on the question, as being in any sense their question; they have given it up in favor of death. But more and more of the spectators have given up on the whole show as being nothing more than a fool show on the wall of Plato's cave. The word now is: Let's get the hell out of here.

TOMORROW

Usually modified by words like "better," "eschatological," "improvement," "hope," "America," all in order to avoid certain simple facts of today. To be taken as symbolic of all those ruses, devices, and chests full of shoddy magic that enable the prestidigitator to distract the householder from the facts of life. Facts: The roof is leaking, the wiring is smoking, the plumbing is flooding the cellar. Every political mock expedient is hammered together and rolled onstage to distract men from their actual and wretched condition. The central truth of that condition is man is where he is; generally without hope, generally without resources. The word is placed here in this glossary a way of underscoring a fact. "Tomorrow" was almost never used by Camus, except in disconcerting juxtaposition to words like *today, now, this man, death, anguish, love, tears, plagues, revolt.*

The hope of Camus was never a device for dislocating man's attention from what is before him; the man at his side, the crisis that summons him to succor others, to expend himself, and possibly to die. The hope of most men in contrast is in the Kingdom of God, even if the Reign of Terror seems its interminable first act. But how shall we be rendered worthy of such a tomorrow?

We are perhaps justified in contrasting, at this point, Camus with Teilhard. After the Bikini test, Teilhard exclaimed that the new bombs "show a humanity which is at peace both internally and externally. They announce the coming of the spirit on earth." Enough said. In these two, Camus and Teilhard, the humanist meets the futurist. And, let it be added, the humanist comes off on certain key attitudes, immeasurably the better.

To some, this will seem an oversimplification. But to others of us, the moral weight attached by the humanist to the condition of man now and here appears immeasurably the more valuable critique of the times we are enduring. Camus spoke often of the "disintoxication" of dreams as part of the process of achieving reality. It is this intoxication of the Jesuit with the triumph of man, even to the point of glossing over his bestial conduct, his nuclear follies, that would most have disturbed Camus. It also might have awakened a debate between two kinds of genius. But it does appear to us that two radically different experiences of human life have led two men, formed by different disciplines and resources, in very different directions. On the one hand, a pedestrian, patient, step-by-step political visionary, who refused all parties and churches; on the other, a sublime, mystical interpreter of the days of wrath, the day of glory. Each will choose for himself which man best speaks for him.

Six

THIS MAN IS ARMED:
THE CLEAVER OF ELDRIDGE

Soul on Ice is an extraordinary book, by all agreement. It is as though the parched soul of the white nation, intent upon self-destruction, had come upon a spring in the desert, stooped over in a paroxysm of disbelief and thirst, and been restored. Consult the best-seller lists.

But this is not the whole story. It does not explain the burning appeal of such a document for young white liberals and radicals. What they discern here is not merely a savage attack, descending with a thump, dividing membrane from bone of the organism they know so well and hate so heartily. Savage attacks, as a matter of fact, are a dime a dozen. What one needs, at this stage of the history of light skins and bleached bones, is precisely an act of faith in the strange and very nearly unbearable experience of being born into a race of post-colonials and present marauders.

An act of faith indeed. If one has a sense of the traditional and honored sense of the word "faith," he understands that its genuine character, as embodied in men like Jeremiah, Jesus, and Paul, is very nearly lost. That is, the sense of the act of faith has something to do with the geography of the act of faith. And it is disturbingly constant throughout the history of what we call faith, that its geography has usually been, from the point of view of whatever establishment, that of an antiworld.

An act of faith indeed. If one wants to study his society,

from the stance of one who can imagine no other society, he goes through the old, weary performance dictated by the Ford Foundation, preordained to failure. That is to say, he wins a grant, and begins to apply the crude, mesmeric instruments of whatever discipline supports his prejudice or his ignorance. Usually, he is pleased, as a kind of voyeur, to turn his sights in the direction of the victims of the society. To study them, to poke and peer into the corners where one has in effect condemned them, has all the charm and titillation of a night on the loose, indulged in by a postcard salesman for Huntington Hartford.

But suppose the end in view is not an academic tour de force, but, quite simply, love. In such a case, a man might well find that his antiworld is a jail cell. And comparing himself to those who make peace with almost any "lesser evil," he may find that he is not antiman at all, but the first man of all. A man so new as almost to be unrecognizable by the old, sorry, savage men who claim the planet and its plunder for themselves and who keep the keys of the jails where imprisoned men are building themselves new, cell upon cell and bone upon bone, in the manner of the old prophet's parable.

If the man in question is a new man, it is quite possible that he invents a new language. And this is the achievement of Cleaver and others. There is no point, if one is going to write in jail, in investing his years in learning or peddling the old recap language of the jailers and pirates outside. Could we then take a look at the vocabulary of Cleaver as a way of getting to the man?

That is why I started to write. To save myself. An interesting clue at the start. The act of salvation is connected with the acts of reading and writing. That is to say, a man is saved when he is literate. He has come to prison as an act of salvation; indeed, his captors may well be his saviors. And in the twentieth century, the first act they have induced in their victim is a purification from all the ways of human speech and language outside. He is now inside. And he must be saved. And being twentieth-century and secular and newly delivered from illiteracy, he realizes that he can be saved by no god; he is required to save himself. He will save himself by becoming conscious—that is to say, by becoming literate. He would like to learn from his antiworld, to read the text of the universe, in its large and small and even its invisible print.

Does this mean merely that up to now, he could not read the Coke signs in the neon jungle he had been plucked from? Obviously, something a little deeper than that. What Cleaver means, I take it, is that he shared, as a matter of social, inevitable inheritance, in the illiteracy of Americans today. As far as reading the text of human life, or of being able to turn within himself, in an act of integral recognition of his own spirit, he found himself as helpless as you or I. Or very nearly so. The difference being that he had broken the law, and might therefore be educable.

The price of hating other human beings is loving oneself less. Indeed, yes. It is a sentence whose spirit rules his book, and helps us to gain a sense of the difference between the hatred that shuts men in cages, and the prophetic hatred that responds to keepers and executioners. We have every reason to believe that Cleaver learned to love and to accept himself in prison. And through that terrible crystal of his own existence, he came to read the text of the bestial lives of those who created the prisons of the world and then populated them with their victims. And whose major activity in the world was invariably one or another analogue to this. Cleaver learned, as the book bears witness, that such major activities are a clue to men's major interior activities; the automurder of Western man, the radical inability of this schizoid to put himself together into one man.

Those whose conscience allows them no better way of living with themselves than the way they live with others, might well take this sentence as a motif for a book of revelations, the book of Cleaver. Such men expect that their victims will proceed to save themselves, according to the same rules and methods by which their executioners have proceeded to destroy themselves.

That is to say, by the outrageous method those in power are pleased to call "civilized discourse." A nice principle indeed, drawn from unimpeachable Greek sources, and adopted almost universally by the little gray men in glasses who make the decisions about the many who shall die and the few who shall live, from Harlem to Hanoi. Rational discourse, indeed; rational discourse gone to seed, sprung up again as gobbledygook.

When the brain of man has rotted in its case, it is not to be rationally thought that he will be capable of rational discourse. So men who are trying to grow in the mind as a crop grows, or a child, try another method. The method has something to do with the soil in which the mind of man grows. The soil today is stony indeed, a combination of prison rock, macadam, ennui, unreason, enclosure, the stifling threat of violence, mindlessness. No matter. What we are talking about is prophetic discourse, fury in the face of repression, a kind of hatred that has nothing to do with the sodden, institutional hatred of the functionary faced with the resistance of real men.

Once I was a Catholic. It is a little like saying, "Once I was a moonchild," or a beanstalk, or a Jack the Ripper. Most of us, in doing something so simple as recalling where we came from, are forced to refer over a period of perhaps twenty years to kinds of former incarnations. Change has been so violent and speedy, our equipment so unready, so unable to catch up and cope, that we hardly can say who we are or where we have come from. The terms are the same: "I was a Catholic"; but the sense of them, the world in which the words are uttered, has changed. "A terrible beauty is born." What has died is by no means so clear.

But you say you were once a Catholic, Cleaver. Then what would you say you are now? A man, perhaps. This it seems to me is exactly the transmigration that the man is trying to speak of. He has gone out of a religious crysalis into a secular world and inhabited that world, a man. He has equated his having been a Catholic with his childhood, and with the temptation to stop there; in spite of the stretching of his own limbs, to remain a child. And so he became a man; this kind of man, who has come from this nest and is no longer within it.

From the point of view of religion, one might ask what sort of faith, what sort of friendships, might have run with the long-distance runner.

All the gods are dead except the god of war. The judgment is so accurate, and comes from such an experience of death, that one is almost silenced in the reading. The context of the statement is Cleaver's discussion of Merton's *The Seven Storey Mountain*, his autobiography. Cleaver was seeking at the time what he calls a world view free of Merton's theism. And he could not find it. It is one of the impossible tragedies of modern life that these two men, so alike in the structure of their souls and the turns of their minds, never met, especially in view of the late development of each. For Cleaver to have judged Merton on the basis of *The Seven Storey Mountain* would be a little like judging Thomas Aquinas by his playpen graffiti.

The first thing I do is make up my bed. The context is his description of a typical day in Folsom Prison. If you make your bed in such a way, you are going to lie in it. Or again, "Take up your bed and walk." We have in the book a tension between inevitability, the killing routine of the prison, which is a kind of bastard Greek sense of the universe; "Nothing can change because nothing ever has changed." And yet, a hint of healing. A man can make something within his skull of such a routine, can close out of his skull all the horrors and harpies wheeling around him, can enter into his spirit as into a forbidden garden. Indeed, he takes up his bed and walks; indeed, since he has made such a bed he must lie in it. But in the resolution of those two, the routine that kills and the discipline that frees, the man becomes a free man.

Books that one wants to read; he won't let you have. The warden says, "No sex," his perpetual squelch. When everything is going downhill in a society, everyone tends to act like everyone else. It is the biggest sign of universal panic. Everyone loses a sense of the life he is living, whether that of censor, secular warden, priest, fireman, Indian chief. The whole careening baggage is running downhill, concentrated in one huge squeal of fear and horror. Something like the sentence here. I am reminded also of the scene when priests invaded the cathedral in Cleveland recently, to protest the Church's silence on the war question. They were surrounded by cops, and those people who were in the church had the delicious experience of hearing a cop move up and down the aisles calling out: "You can leave now, your Sunday obligation has been fulfilled."

When everything is going to hell, cardinals tend to talk like generals, generals give homilies, cops patrol churches. And a few men get liberated; a very few.

I felt I could endure anything, everything, even the test of being broken on the rack. A man's assessment of his life comes out of the life he is leading, if the assessment is to have any value at all. It would be rewarding to dig into the mix of exhilaration, rock will, and boiling resentment that makes a man ready to put his soul on ice, for years, for others. You have to be in a certain skin, you have to be in a certain skull. And the best way to tell where you are is to be where you are: really be there, a man; not a cooped animal, but a man in his own skull and skin. Thank you, Eldridge, wherever you are; the cleaver hurts.

"I guess you heard about Malcolm?" "Yeah," I said. "They say he got wasted." Wasted seed, wasted blood, wasted passionate insight, foresight, hindsight, wasted new untranslatable (by most) love, wasted prophecy, wasted steely hell cat glances, wasted surgical (free) operations on the wasted minds of the mentally ill racist millions. Wasted guts, wasted nurture of the poor. O man we miss you, a big gap in the ecology; polluted air, polluted water—pollution of heroes. Waste of war, the best downed first. "How long, how many years, to make a man; how brief, how easy, how quick to destroy him!" (Péguy, *Passion of Joan.*)

I find that a rebirth does not follow automatically, of its own accord. So, indeed, do most of us find; the biology of that deed, the making of a man, does not follow upon the induced spasm in the organism of a mother, much less upon the intricate meshing and tripping of a machine. . . . The analogy with other processes, in the case of the spirit, is always from the lesser to the greater. As we love to say. What we love to act on is something else again. A simple test might be (instance): Who of us risks his life for his brother? or, Whose umbilical is connected to anyone, except to the bodies of his kids or his mother? And yet the umbilical is an analogy. And so do animals connect with their mothers and their young. . . . And if this is still the ruling limit of love (care of the young, the call of the blood), why not organize society along the model of the zoo, and have done with it (a fairly efficient system, with controls, imperatives, seasonal sex, territories, feeding, discipline, strictly utilitarian violence—all built in by a vigilant, lynx-eyed nature)?

What has suddenly happened is that the white race has lost its heroes. A statement of immeasurable import. The sentence is dumped in our laps; take it from there. That is to say, in the haunted house where the illegitimate white heroes have ruled (shotguns from the windows, the mad, inbred squire), something else may be going on too. A white hero may be getting born. . . . But first, let the old heroes die; they have marauded long enough. And let us think in the meantime, and draw in the meantime, formulas for new heroes, from the nonwhite world around. For example: Could we have imagined H. C. Minh (holding equivalent power with the Russians or Americans) sending the marines into some nearby Cuba, some nearby Czechoslovakia? I could not. Can you imagine S. Carmichael (holding equivalent power to R. Nixon) prolonging the Vietnam war for a single day? I cannot. Can you imagine Dom Helder Camara (holding equivalent power to Paul VI) publishing a letter like *Of Human Life?* (Bondage?) I cannot. Can you imagine, for that matter, any conceivable coalition of the poor throughout the world, any political arrangement fostered by the developing peoples, tolerating the American military budget for a single hour? Nor can I.

It is the struggle that makes the heroes. Cleaver is right, his impatience is right; there are not enough years left to make a hero in the old way. In the press, under the millstones, it can be done in a single hour. Black struggle makes black heroes; white struggle makes white heroes. The whites are called to struggle for liberation from bankrupt forms of power (name one of them that is not bankrupt) in state and church, economics and family and foreign policy and education and the military. All the ways (very nearly all) of being a man that we inherited and were born into and baptized under are finished. We call it alienation: correct. Liberation from tired heroes, clairvoyance to see and cast off—F. D. Roosevelt, Pius XII, W. Churchill, E. Hemingway, P. Picasso, C. de Gaulle. And reaching back farther in your history (which we had considered unassailable and pure, the creation of good men), freedom from Minute Men and frontiersmen and slave traders and gold rushers and tycoons and railroad builders and ward bosses and bishops and ambassadors and the Rockefellers and Harrimans (the latest H. said in Paris to Tom Hayden: now I see that we are morally superior to the North Vietnamese) and the Fords (watch them go by—for good). Ten years, five years have brought down the heroic statuary that some 150 years of national history had built. The scaffolding was scarcely removed, and the statue is down in a single night; brought down by that time bomb that we name time itself, or more properly, human consciousness. The king is naked, the fool is savior.

There is, of course, no shortcut for this new form of consciousness. Young white men and women learned at the Pentagon in autumn of '67, at Columbia in the following May, and again on the streets of Chicago. In the meantime, the struggle continues. The young whites, the young draft resisters, the young SDS activists, students, priests, nuns are winning the respect of their black opposite numbers, even from a distance, the distance that separates the descendants of slaves from the descendants of slave masters. Distance with respect. And I suspect that the distance will diminish as the respect grows.

I saw recently in a black newspaper in Boston a cartoon; three accused men stand before a single white judge: Rap Brown, Huey Newton, and Philip Berrigan. The ground of the struggle becomes clear and common. It is a no-man's-land rendered uninhabitable by napalm, defoliants, blockbusters, antipersonnel bombs, slums, Daley's cops, military proving grounds, Humphrey's tomfooling, Nixon's tricks, Bikini experiments, Johnson's jungle. A no-man's-land created by inhuman men. This is the common ground we seek to claim and clear—for one another with one another. To know that the world belongs neither to the beasts nor the war-makers nor the colonialists nor the Russians nor the Americans nor the first families nor the slave masters nor the corporations. It belongs to the people. "And on the sixth day God created man. To His own image He created him. And He said, 'Multiply and prosper and fill the earth.' And so it was done. And the Lord saw that it was good." How much travail ahead?

I think of the white man's plight. We are being thrust in white skins into the bullcage of black suffering; and this is the world: prison, defamation, illegal overkill, kangaroo courts. Before the war hotted up, the federal prison at Allenwood (one among many) was predominantly black. In the space of one year, with the same number of blacks, it is predominantly white. It is filled with the young draft resisters and Jehovah's Witnesses. No privacy, over-loaded facilities, white Jehovah's Witnesses and white Christians. What a change of scene! What a change of consciousness! The black percentage is shifting. The center of gravity is shifting. The cost of being man is marked upon both skins—at least by way of first installment.

The moral equivalent of being a man has not been realized by white men. We are only just beginning to discover it. And our discovery amounts to being accounted as felons in a white society—destroyers of idols, iconoclasts, burners of war records. How could I be a man when I was condemned to be a white man? I could only seek out, as best I might, a way of being a just man. I could refuse to kill, refuse to pay taxes, refuse to be institutionalized, refuse to be obedient, refuse to be silent, refuse to die where I have been born. I could refuse to accept all those claims on me that kept me white—whitewashed, a white sepulcher, white and therefore powerful, white and therefore right. I had to get where the action is; or to borrow a biblical term, I had to get where the passion is.

All of this, of course, is hard. We have lived and died so long without heroes. We are asked to create them, but there is virtually no example of white twentieth-century man living in the world, becoming conscious in a white skull, enduring the humiliation of ersatz freedom, refusing the benefits of inherited colonialism, speaking the truth to corrupt power, urging the facts of life upon the deluded.

"It is not a time for building justice," wrote my brother from prison, "it is a time for confronting injustice." Say no! The "No" makes the hero.

Part Three

CORNELL

CORNELL: TWO POEMS

One

ARRIVAL, 1967

Coming opens a chasm.
I think both of the Lord's
and a woman's body; invention
(literally) by spike or rod
mothers life. Father broods
like a waylaying cloud above
waters he struck open.

The university falls away forever;
its gift numbs like a cataract
lisps like an undergraduate's
numbers. Choose your entailing
season, read as you run.

I come like the moon
crossing the chasm
a footless midnight
trespasser on Triphammer bridge.
Indeed, a feeble passage after
sun all day struck sparks like shod hooves—
intelligence, panoply of artists
genius, enteleche.
                    The bells
make passion logical. Stone on stone

rising, water on waters pausing
falling, a law of minds;
                              above
shekinah, the glory of God
                                   beneath
here and there
pools, cold, untouchable
wisdom
            the sun never
X's like doomed trees
                              for the torrid
glance of its ax

Two

TORMENT, 1969

Today six elderly mandarins, resorting to the N. Y. Times
    (that last infirmary of gray minds)
    proclaimed: Academic Freedom Still Exists at Cornell!

They quote Socrates to no purpose; like Homer's old men
    manning the wrong battlement, a buzzing of locusts.
        Their lives, like this;

—they come down like deities on wires
    from segregated heavens, befoul the dust
with this or that exhausted tradition

        then are hauled up, out of sight and mind
    the heavens closing like a trap. *Requiescat!*
Everything said and done. In SDS heads
    sanity scrambles like eggs

    the big graffiti on construction fences
erase overnight, an op nightmare.
        Insolvency, despairing wit; student busted
    (an image of rag dolls, cops breaking like dry sticks
Jehovah's cunning handiwork)

The ivy frets and crawls like poison ivy
    infecting the solid battlements of mind
    breaking that Hanseatic League to bits.

O John Harvard, Messrs. Brown and Yale
    original sin, your transplant, rottens the public heart
Ezra Cornell turns watery where he stands
    his land grant sours, his piracies
bring in no cash. O foundering father!

Three

CORNELL, 1969:
MANCHILD IN THE POISON IVY

I

BYERS:* You were here during the time the blacks were occupying Willard Straight Hall at Cornell. Could you briefly describe the scene as you found it?

BERRIGAN: I think the most profitable way to begin would be
to discuss the issues that led to the seizure of the Student Union.
For those who were trying to read the text, events had been
gathering to a head for quite a while. The immediate issue that
faced the black community in its history of frustration and neglect at Cornell was the judiciary. That structure of "justice" reflected the attitude of Cornell toward the black community,
toward social change, and toward those who would challenge the
accepted conduct of white brahmins. One must also insist, if he
is to be just toward what followed, that the university was totally
unprepared for political change or indeed even for political activity.

The judiciary was set up about ten years ago as a way of
summoning students charged with petty campus violations. It
was, in essence, a structure designed to keep the domestic peace
of Alma Mom. Obviously, such a judiciary was not prepared for

---

* [Tom Byers, a student at Cornell and a member of SDS, taped this
conversation with Father Berrigan in order to record their impressions
of the Cornell confrontation that took place in the spring of 1968.]

anything like mature political action that would break the peace and threaten to drive Mom out of her head. The blacks unfortunately had no moms, urging them, by instruments of affection and subsidy, to keep the peace. (Even Moynihan at that time, was capable of seeing that.) No subsidies. They were ghetto blacks. As such, they were desperate for political change.

Meantime, back on the plantation (Cornell has an enormous plantation), the platonic game continued. It was a game by whose rules all nonwhite students—black, brown, yellow, or red—were presumed ready to play, by the grace of admission.

Cornell let the blacks in, got the money for them, made a new game possible for—them. Now, could the university be required to enter into serious discussion about the sources of its power, its curriculum, its style? It was somewhat as though students had suddenly announced as a simple fact that God did not exist, or that the bureaucracy of Cornell was behind the times (practically speaking, a like blasphemy). Or that the university was racist. Or that it was unfitted for a totally new cultural adventure.

To put it simply, Cornell, like other large universities, was quite unprepared for the assault of change. The judiciary process that summoned the blacks for accounting was one symbol of the unwillingness of the university to accept social change as a fact of life. And change was what struck, like a fist in the belly, in the spring of 1969. Students from the urban ghettos were suddenly to unmask the countenance of the American university (as a sign of the unpreparedness of American society; the blacks insisted on the parallel), its unwillingness to accept human beings who might have something to say about the uses and distribution of power. Let the fact be noted: The blacks wanted the university to survive. They saw that its survival was important for their own survival. So they occupied the Student Union, unarmed, one spring morning, having specifically chosen the weekend when parents of university students come to enjoy the pleasures of the unspoiled playground.

The blacks chose their time and place deliberately in order

to dramatize, I would think, the larger betrayal, neglect, and blindness at work against them. That is to say, the university was living in the nineteenth century, on Ivy League suppositions, isolated spiritually and physically, thriving on the sweat and tears of the poor, both locally and throughout the world. Its style was a clue to the conduct of the whole society. This is a harsh indictment. We will try to document it as we go along.

Question: You had been here at Cornell for about two years. During that time what was the Afro-American Society doing to attempt to change the university structure, that it might deal in a more relevant way with the issues?

Answer: This was one of the things the black students tried desperately to make clear after their seizure of the building. They tried to say they had not acted arbitrarily; they had not come to an extreme act, without trying at every level to approach the university and to make clear the inadequacies of university structures.

As long ago as spring of 1968, the black students had sought access to heads of departments, deans, vice presidents, and the president himself, in order to protest certain classes that they found to be racist. They got nowhere. That episode culminated in the seizure of the office of the head of the Economics Department. The blacks held this office for five hours; several vice presidents eventually agreed, under pressure, to bargain about points the blacks considered to be points of survival.

The next significant step occurred around Christmas of 1968. A black girl was ordered evicted from a dormitory because she was using inflammatory language toward fellow students. The black students were ready. They barricaded a vice president's office until they were assured that the girl would have access to a black psychiatrist, and would not be evicted from the university on medical grounds without recourse. I think it necessary to underscore a fact; the black students understood that in so acting, they were vindicating the rights of all students. It had been a long-standing rule at Cornell that the word of medical "experts" was sufficient to effect dismissal of a student from the university, without outside opinion. The black students refused to tolerate so arbitrary a rule; it was they who stood ground. They declared they were struggling for the right of appeal in behalf of all students, in cases that were bound to be complicated and delicate. They won easily, a victory whose implications for the future were already clear.

Toward the spring of 1969, black students were again under fire. They had indulged in a kind of guerrilla theater earlier in the winter; they invaded the library, the Student Union, and a coffee house, and disrupted the activity there. In this way, they dramatized their feeling that centers of university service were irrelevant to their needs. As a consequence, they were drummed before the judiciary; and it was at this point that the mortal weakness of the judicial system began to be felt. For years there had been only *loco parentis* cases to be dealt with. But here was a new and ominous sign—disruptive political actions, understandable only if one had a feeling for deep historical wrongs and the passion that their neglect had engendered. At least some of us at Cornell began to ask ourselves: Is it possible for the university to find ways of dealing with new kinds of action and with students who are despairing of institutional change? We still have no answer. Or, rather, we have no real hope of an affirmative answer.

BYERS: Many people, when they read reports of the "spring offensive" at Cornell, find the issue of separate "black studies" programs somewhat confusing. I wonder if you would go into some of the problems that make such a department particularly relevant to Cornell.

BERRIGAN: It is difficult to interpret the hopes and anguish of people whom white history has placed at an enormous spiritual distance. It is almost as though an Earthman were trying to talk about his life to Martians. After all, we stand at the far end of 250 years of murderous racism, near the outcome of that history. We are trying to act out in our generation the difference between the slave master's son and the son of the slave, both of whom long for an end to slavery. And this is a very difficult thing.

First because the son of the slave is not anxious to talk to us. He is at a point where the existence of his community, with its powerlessness, is a life-and-death question. And that is a very different thing than the situation of five years ago, when whites went into the South with SNCC and CORE to "help create justice for black people." We are at a new stage of things. Now we are trying, across silence, anger, and intrusion into "our property," to discover what black students want as a black community. They are not at all interested in talking to us about what they want, except by way of demands and reparations. It is quite clear that a new stage of consciousness has arrived; one of its signs is the unwillingness of blacks to share a slice of their consciousness. That is to say, they are no longer interested in announcing to us, as a negotiable factor, their determination to live, even in our midst, as human beings. They believe that apart from property and power, we have nothing to offer them. We may have something to offer one another, but that is not the present question.

When SNCC went south in '65, white northern students, with the best intentions, were leading black people in voting registration drives, out of cotton fields and sharecroppers' cabins, into towns and county seats. These black people had never done anything in their lives except obey white people. Now they were obeying them again. For any black person who realized the implication of all this, it was clear that such a situation would not do. It could not be considered encouraging that black people, coming out of poverty and ignominy and a history of slavery, should decide once more to obey whites (this time, white liberals) in order to get registered as political equals. And this is what we are talking about.

Northern white liberals were murdered in the South; their deaths attracted attention, chiefly among northern white liberals. But the neglected fact was that the murder of blacks in the South had gone unnoticed for 250 years. (And this is where we are too.) Suddenly, between 1965 and 1968, a change of the greatest import occurred. At that point the revolution moved north.

It said "no" to the intrusion of whites upon any black scene, North or South.

"Pacify the natives," a good liberal formula, was ended. Murder had gone on too long, exclusion too long, rhetoric too long, co-option too long. Something new was in the air. The natives were growing restless—restless as hell. And so the scene shifted to another "restricted playground" area—the northern Ivy League campus—to Cornell. The university began its first effort, in the summer of 1966, to increase black student enrollment. The supposition was clear to those who could read. The white campuses of the North, basking in their mellow history, had gone largely unchallenged in all that history; no serious questioning of suppositions. They seemed to lie beyond scrutiny or challenge; a prestigious avenue of advance, a fun house, a laboratory, a home away from home, a shrine of secular hopes. Might northern universities also become the scene of black advance? Might not the *penetralia* be opened to blacks also, after serious screening, testing of neophytes, the undergoing of purification rites? Indeed, yes; for we are a generous people.

So it was done. Before the fact, there was, of course, no way of grasping the possibility that things might turn out badly. The blacks might even turn on their benefactors. Unthinkable! Throw sand in the elaborate expensive machinery that granted escalation into the Best of All Societies? The Best Possible Trustees, relying on the Best Advice Available, were agreed: gratitude, industry, virtuous conduct might realistically be expected, as Enlightenment proceeded. The blacks were admitted.

The fact is, of course, that Cornell, like every other northern campus, was totally unprepared to take black students aboard. Mutiny? On the S.S. *Bounty?* Alas. Only three years after her decision, in the spring of 1969, Cornell reaped the fruit of unpreparedness. I am convinced that the harvest, bitter as it is, is not the fruit of malice. It is simply that white men and their institutions are unready for any vision of man that is not white; they are unready for any culture that is not white, right, and therefore mighty. That is to say, the culture is racist in principle and conduct—which is to define, among other excellent institutions, Cornell University.

Question: What were the goals of the blacks' political actions during 1968 and 1969 at Cornell, regarding the restructuring of the university?

Answer: I think that that question is, of all questions, possibly the most neglected, the least understood, and the most ridden with mythology. Consequently it is constantly mauled by the public media. With this question we touch upon what I conceive to be the inability of white society to apprehend what is really working (in the sense of yeast, ferment, principle of newness) in its own radical youth. That is the first point. Whites are in confusion before their own sons and daughters. Is it to be wondered at that black language, style, and power inhabit the white mind like a noonday nightmare?

The blacks have a vision, a program—in a manner of speaking, a modest utopia. During the week following the seizure of the Student Union I was involved in a series of panel discussions at the Veterinary School of Cornell, one of the most isolated areas of the campus, one of the schools most in control of an unchanging faculty. During that week, the veterinary students gathered their courage and invited a panel of three black students, previously involved in the seizure of the Student Union, to speak to them. The atmosphere was alive with torment and expectation. Could black students respond to an opposite current of feeling? The question was by no means an abstract one.

Neither was the answer. They could. They presented, in an unassailing and nonviolent way, an understanding of things that went far beyond the campus. They talked knowledgeably about the Third World, about the poor of Ithaca and the Tompkins County area surrounding and affected by the university. And this, I submit, is a clue to the violence, obsession, egoism, and frenzy that seized the campus during those days and was transmitted through the public media. The black students spoke very calmly of their aims: a Harlem college in New York, decent housing, controlled by the poor, for the poor of the area, a reasonable measure of student autonomy in the university. They noted that their struggle was joined to the struggle against war and racism; to the odious realities fostered by Cornell investments in South Africa, as well as the business connections of university trustees throughout the Third World. It was an astonishing leap of consciousness; these young people realized in effect that if their struggle was limited only to their own interests, it was doomed from the beginning. The worth of human action was one's moral stance before the world. The black students spoke in this way, with dignity and dispassion. By the end of the evening, it could be seen that they had made their point. They also had seriously disturbed the semi-conscious state of students who never in their lives had thought of the fate of other people—the community "outside the walls," the peoples of other continents, the implications of dwelling in a university paradise, while accepting little or no responsibility for the fate of the majority of men.

Question: Would you discuss the measures that were taken against the action of the black students? And what about the immediate goals of the seizure of the Student Union?

Answer: Here comes the sixty-four-dollar one: the question of the faculty of the university as a powerful influence upon the exclusion, control, or acceptance of student political action.

Involved here, as it turned out within a few days after the seizure, was the picayune nature of the issue before the Faculty Council and the judiciary. What inflated the issue out of all proportion was faculty honor and image; faculty control of Cornell, in sum. It was quite clear that summoning blacks to face a judicial process for their two hours of guerrilla fun-making was beside the point. As became clear at a later faculty meeting, it was irrelevant before the law whether the blacks showed up at all. They could as well have been judged in absentia, according to Cornell rules. But the faculty had created a primary issue; given the faculty, there could be no backing off. Unless the blacks showed up for their slap on the wrist, they would be displaying bad faith and should be doubly condemned. Here was the issue, in this life-and-death year of our Lord, 1969. Is it any wonder that the human spirit grew depressed, and our hopes dampened, as we viewed the spectacle of some twelve hundred civilized, supposedly eminent men, conducting their game with all the rigor mortis seriousness of a morticians' convention?

But to go back a bit. The blacks had had recourse to the judiciary over a period of months, to try to awaken a debate on main issues; that is to say, the distinction between traditional student malfeasance and responsible, though disruptive, political action. The faculty had never admitted such a distinction. Its political savvy was, in fact, at the level of an Arkansas circuit judge. So the faculty persisted in dealing with political activists as though they had been Saturday night law breakers, speeding through campus, disrupting dormitory life, or disturbing the Sabbath peace. But the idea that students should become politically responsible, should assail faculty, administration, and fellow students alike with the news of world and national change—the issues were never accepted in such terms.

The faculty thus made the seizure of a building, or some like action, inevitable. After all areas of recourse failed, and the university showed itself unwilling, unable, or despairing in face of real grievances, suddenly, in a political move of the highest order and thoughtfulness, black students entered the Student Union, on Saturday, May 3, 1969.

BYERS: The number of supporters outside the Straight grew from the original fifty or so SDS pickets to several thousand students and faculty during the seizure. Could you describe the growth of consciousness that occurred on campus during the seizure?

BERRIGAN: Practically everyone who was part of any university movement was involved in the events of the weekend. And that is a measure of the growth the black students induced in us.

Maybe we can take events hour by hour as they occurred. From nine until eleven o'clock Saturday morning, the campus was leafleted by white students in support of the seizure at six o'clock that morning. There were calls to mass meetings in support of the blacks, calls to picket in front of the Student Union, summonses to attention upon what was beyond doubt a moment of history for all. For all of us; this was the fact to be understood. On other campuses this spring, notably at CCNY, white students had been turned in a different direction; things had not gone well after this or that black action. But as the outcome showed, the action of the Cornell blacks was correct. It contributed to sanity and growth and patience; it was part of the revolutionary long haul. The whites were ready, in varying degrees of understanding—except, of course, for a few neanderthals who would never in principle be ready for anything.

But from midmorning of Saturday until forty hours later, the white community at Cornell lay low, hypersensitive to what was occurring within the mysterious barred precincts of the Student Union, suddenly declared off-bounds. That building became a focal point not merely for the campus, but for the nation and the world. Cornell had arrived. That is to say, the intellectual and spiritual presuppositions of 250 years of white history were suddenly brought to a burning point. History was focused to a moment; from it, rays of heat and light were burning away our impurities and cowardice. We, the people who also wanted change, set up a picket line and called mass meetings. We began a long effort to interpret this sudden onslaught of history. We invited the parents who remained on campus throughout the two days to search with us for a measure of understanding. Temperatures continued to rise. A few white troglodytes decided to invade the Straight on Saturday morning, to counter what they were pleased to see as "nigger uppityness," with their own type of violence. Shortly thereafter, they were evicted noisily into the hands of medicine men, and the main event went on. But one fact had become clear; the intrusion had tightened the coil to the point where white violence was being met by preparations for self-defense on the part of the blacks.

(The coil was further wound on Saturday night, when a campus fraternity house suddenly went up in flames. In an atmosphere already approaching insanity, word went around that the blacks had set upon whites. In fact, the mishap was due to something as innocuous as malfunctioning electrical equipment.) But during that weekend, it seems as though everything conspired to turn the consciousness of sane men away from real meaning and real tasks. Indeed, could sane men concentrate upon the meaning of the building occupation, and respond to it sanely? Could we show solidarity with it, as an act of conscience, an act that might lead us beyond our impasse? The answer was not clear.

B Y E R S : As the seizure went on, the campus became aware of what was happening, and in a short time many different factions claimed their share of attention. Could you describe, first of all, the role that the SDS played during and after the seizure?

B E R R I G A N : SDS, blacks, conservatives, faculty, religious gurus, everyone rushed into costume. I think one of the lessons that came home was the very large part the irrational played in events of the weekend. The university had always proceeded on the assumption that it alone was the spokesman for rational men. The rhetoric went this way: question leads to answer, assumption leads to verification, convergence of evidence leads to proof. Fear not! The rational mind, in command of white Western history for two thousand years, is still in command.

In fact, almost the exact opposite was true. Events of Western history were in motion, soundless and slow as an iceberg melting in a warming sea. Other forces were converging, another mass than the mind was setting the temperature of things. Poets and playwrights and artists, beatniks and blacks and copouts and hippies, revolutionaries and dreamers and martyrs, these were determining the future, the massive meaning of man that lay below the surface of rational intellect. Was another definition of man emerging?

To be a-rational is not to be antirational; on the other hand, to be committed, in a sterilized, selfish way, to the life of the intellect, is to bring the mind and its proper function very near to ruin. I would contrast here the activity of those who understood the real forces at work in time of crisis, with those committed to the past as the only measure of the future. What happens to men who literally cannot imagine any form of life but the one they have known? I would think that the SDS was the finely honed edge of white change, here as elsewhere. The differences at Cornell was that the SDS had subjected itself for some two or three years to a process of patient, ongoing change. And that meant a very great difference in the resources it could bring to bear when the point of crisis was reached. The Cornell SDS did not go off in the insane byways of the chapter at Columbia. The Cornell SDS identified itself in the main with those forces of patience and community effort that had won the admiration and support of the community over the last years. Very concretely, the SDS organized. It surrounded the Student Union with large numbers of students and faculty, to protect the occupying blacks from possible violence. I pay tribute to the civilized and humane resources of SDS, its historical rightness, its understanding of what was really operating in our midst. SDS determined to protect, to interpret, and to further the efforts of the black brothers to achieve a community that would be worthy of whatever future might emerge.

A mark of historical validity struck me on that night as hundreds of us reflected, in the cold, on what was occurring within the occupied building. A group of white students, intent for several years upon what they considered valid social change, was able to meet a moment of history precipitated by another group. SDS and the blacks had never before shared a common hope. Each kept strictly to its own turf, by common agreement. This strikes me as crucial; on the night of the building seizure SDS passed whatever test could be applied to a responsible community. They realized that history had gathered around the blacks. White men could be expected to surround and protect others, to nurture and interpret their action for the sake of the larger community. And this is to the glory of SDS; it represented the best, most conscientious forces then operating at

Cornell. I say this with full deliberation. I mean to exclude the faculty, the administration, and those middle forces that were able only later to borrow their vitality from the example of SDS.

B Y E R S : Three of us, on duty outside the Straight, were among those rotating in shifts, responsible for holding off the curiosity seekers, the furious, or the drunken or confused. Late that night, we went over to Chi Psi to have a look at the fraternity house fire. When we arrived, we found on the outskirts of the group many fraternity people muttering that the blacks had set the fire. The talk was dangerous, ridden with fear and rumor. We stayed and talked with those people. Finally it emerged that the fire had in fact started in an elevator; it was a problem of electrical wiring.

It was also interesting to note that among those guarding the Straight, many offered their houses to people who were burned out and needed shelter for the night. The fraternity people were very grateful for the help. But still, a kind of fringe hysteria attended the rumors that bore down on the blacks, adding to the general hysteria that pervaded the community. When we returned to the Straight I remember standing in the rain with a small group of friends. We were very tired and cold and confused by the incidents that had taken place. Just then I looked up and saw one of the blacks standing on a balcony of the Straight, three stories up. I made out his silhouette there; in his hand was what appeared to be a long stick. Then an SDS brother, at my side, told me that the blacks now had arms; what I was seeing was in reality a gun.

I can remember the fear that came over me; we had heard of fraternity people arming themselves, drinking heavily, riding around in the night. Now the blacks, in self-defense, had armed themselves. And here we were, standing in the middle ground between these two. And the thought struck me; this seems a kind of metaphor for the way the social scene in America was going. The position of the white radical American lay somewhere between the forces of the emerging world and the America he had been born into.

Another event of that day was a gathering of parents and fraternity people at Noyes Center. An assistant professor was holding a kind of kangaroo court, ostensibly reviewing events since the seizure. In fact, he was trying the blacks in *absentia*. He welcomed testimony from several of the fraternity boys who had broken into the building earlier in the day, and from several parents who had been evicted from the Student Union at dawn. The professor was encouraging a one-sided estimate of the solution. And I had a feeling of horror, seeing a kind of insanity, labeled as rational thinking, being handed out to the press and the parents on campus, as if it were honest and objective opinion. But when I tried to speak, I was shouted down. As a matter of fact, one student came up, pinned me against the wall, and started shouting at me. He had been in the fraternity whose members had tried to attack the black students in the occupied building early that morning. A campus chaplain finally managed to win a little ground. But I was struck by the fact that the parents were more irrational and upset, and behaved in a worse way, than their sons and daughters. And this, I think, is some slight consolation; things, bad as they are, are actually improving.

BERRIGAN: Of course, the parents were much less prepared for the turbulent, up-close scene than the students were. Those students who were hep to anything at all must have known that something was in the wind, after the long effort of both black and white radicals to win some measure of change on campus. But the parents on campus were traditionally those who came to be reassured about the status of their sons and daughters. If one could push their credentials farther, almost by supposition the parents had "made it." They came from segregated neighborhoods and had a stake in the "two societies" spoken of in the Kerner report. Such people would therefore look upon the university as the outer reach of their own effort to inhibit change on their own turf.

The parents who stayed on for the weekend were suddenly

exposed to what was occurring elsewhere; not only in ghettos
and on campuses, but in the lives of their sons and daughters.
The forty-eight hours of Cornell's trauma might even be considered a kind of gift to the parents. They were transported, like
it or not, into the realities of American life, 1969—transported
bodily out of the myths and illusions operative in what they were
pleased to call their "way of life" at home.

On Sunday morning, a series of meetings was hastily set up
between the parents and the university community. Anyone who
wanted to talk with the parents about the weekend turmoil took
part. We met from about ten in the morning until midafternoon
in various parts of the campus. The parents, as quickly became
clear, were for the most part pure American. I remember how
several of them arose in righteous wrath to declare their outrage
at the dawn evictions from the Student Union. One of them
went on to employ a classic parallel to justify his anger and
frustration. On the Thruway from New York, the state police
stopped him for speeding. He realized, as he pulled over, that he
had broken the law; he was quite ready to admit his wrongdoing
and to accept the penalty. And he offered this ideal attitude as
an example of what any "law-abiding American" ought to be
ready for in the face of law violation. In fact, he continued
heatedly, on Saturday morning the law had been broken at
Cornell. And why, he shouted, were not the blacks ready to pay
the penalty for breaking the law, as he had realized his guilt
on the Thruway the previous morning?

It was a very difficult and patient process to try to lead this
man to see a crucial difference: the experience of blacks trying
to gain redress for long-standing, visible wrongs, and a minor
violation for which a white burgher was expected later to pay a
minor fine, and thereupon proceed to business as usual, no questions asked. Could one expect that such a man, or indeed the
university, would be ready to catch up with some 250 years of
neglected history? Would such people be ready to concede that
the university and the society were wrongdoers of long standing,

or that the crimes of society, prolonged in inheritance, possession, and immunity, were coming due for payment?

Well, it was a very heated and long exchange. And I am not at all sure that it got anywhere. But at least it was one of the few efforts we could extend to an older generation: telling the truth about the society out of which the parents had come and to which the students would return. Let it be stated simply; the parents, by and large, were racist. They were strangers to the facts of social change, to the revenge that was following hard upon the long neglect of social justice. How to bring home to them the truth about the neighborhoods they left, the jobs they were holding, the expectations they entertained concerning their children? This was, indeed, a very large order of education for one weekend. One could only hope that a certain unease had been created; the parents might perhaps return to the war-making, exploitative society somewhat less convinced of the religious and civic rightness of their lives. Or so one could hope.

BYERS: At Noyes Center, when I was exchanging with the parents, I felt that their vision of their children and of the university was outmoded and altogether inaccurate. The university stood at the far end of a series of nursery schools; valid political change had nothing to do with its function. Therefore, the action of the blacks could not be considered serious. It occurred in a nursery school, to which children came, by supposition, to be instructed, entertained, and disciplined. Nothing more. And this was very enlightening to me. I felt that the geography of change, the shifting roles of young and old in our society, and the pressures and awakening of youth, were all being illumined by the behavior of the parents. They were treating the university as if it were a scene out of a comic strip, because, as many of us came to understand, the parents themselves were somewhat like comic strip characters. They were shouting the words we come to expect of people who are trite and irrelevant, completely out of touch with the cutting edge of change as it is descending on our universities.

BERRIGAN: I was thinking also of the expectation the parents were voicing, consciously or not. The conviction was implicit in their words that the real task of a worthy son or daughter was to repeat the style of life of their parents. Be like us! was the first commandment. The young people were forbidden to pass over any bridge that would join them to a new scene. But for a son to declare that a life style may once have been right, but was now finished; or right, but used up; or right, but subject to criticism—this was totally unacceptable. Was a son allowed to insist that public affluence should also include the hopes of a black man, or a black community? That was a sin against sources; it violated the biology.

Now, in the face of all this, it seemed to me that the young people were trying to say something entirely different, something like this: "To include black hopes, black power, black community is to declare ourselves truly, perhaps for the first time, sons of our parents and of our society. It is also a way of negating the sin that accompanied our birth." It was an old biblical theme: To get rid of the original sin of slavery, under which our birth had occurred, we must move in friendship and risk to join the quest of our black brothers' freedom. Horrors! Such a view of things is unacceptable by supposition; the Vietnam war continues, racism is in command, the military controls the economy. The original sin is constantly validated. That is to say, the society moves on the supposition that the nonwhite, non-Western world is enslaved in fact and expendable in principle. It is as simple as that.

But suddenly our own sons are saying, "No." The former slaves are our brothers; we shall become their brothers in unmasking the enslavement of our parents. The generation gap is indeed upon us.

BYERS: Facing the parents and watching them and their response to the whole situation, I learned a great deal about the schizophrenia that rules the minds of most Americans, particularly the older ones. According to them, the university is a place where their children are taught sacred things. It is a sacred institution, apart from the cares and troubles and threats of every-

day life. It is an institution on hallowed ground, set aside for
truly objective, rational approaches to human life. They cannot
face the events that of late, at Harvard, Berkeley, and Cornell,
are showing the true face of the university, the truth about society.
And as soon as their sons' convictions begin to threaten the
parents' suppositions, they revolt against their own. The field
of force is altered; we have a white struggle, as Cleaver saw,
arising in the white tribe. This is the American dilemma that is
particularly inherent in the parent-son crisis. It amused me to see
these parents behave as if the greatest moral question facing
college students were a question of obedience. But we hear a
different drummer. We are not here to decide whether to obey
the precepts they hand down to us; we are here to test those
precepts. And when we do this in the college situation, they want
out, and they want us out. In the light of day, affection, calls to
loyalty, protestations of love, tears even, are exposed as a sham.
Our parents can't take us.

BERRIGAN: It seems to me that parents think first of life as
a task, and then announce it to their sons as a last-ditch loyalty.
Parents begin by saying: Our first task is to make a decent human
life for ourselves and our children. Obedience is only on the
edge of their vision. But suddenly, as at Cornell, they are confronted with the reality: The "task" idea of life is highly questionable. To make one's place in the sun is suddenly a dark,
questionable project. Why? Who says so? The children refuse to
continue a process that has somehow been made into a loyalty
test. Parents are insisting to their children, in a thousand ways,
including bribes and rewards, you are supposed to honor our
lives by living as we lived, because we are your parents and
because we are right. This same task, transferred to you, is now
a test of obedience. . . . And the sons say "no"; simply, unequivocally. Therefore, in the eyes of the parents, the sons are
disobedient; they are insisting that the task of a decent life must
be defined in a new way, that the new way must include the
victims who have paid for our *dolce vita.*

BYERS: It is a question of threatening an entire generation's immortality; undermining, washing out those suppositions and products they created within their own lifetime. This is an exceedingly difficult thing for older people to face and to get with. How few parents will say, "Although I am forty-five or fifty, I will build with you. I will leave the old road to help you build a new one because we have come to the end of the old road." They talk about a generation gap; it means that parents simply cannot face the questions surrounding their own bid for immortality and truth. What is a man worth? The question suddenly has nothing to do with income or bank account. It has to do with quality of life.

BERRIGAN: I think that in talking about the parents we are still discussing the university somewhat in this way. The life of the mind, as it tries to realize itself in an explosive social scene, borrows its metaphor from biology, but is not enslaved to it. That is to say, the mind cannot afford, any more than the parent can, to be platonic. The mind must move; it must accept new forms of community, new demands for decency and justice that arise in the very course of growth itself. The parent who is enslaved to the past says; the best thing my children can do is to reproduce my life, since I am obviously decent and just and have created something good for those who follow. But the sons and daughters must declare a rebellion, almost in the nature of things. They must say, in effect, the past is applicable only in proportion as it includes new forms of life, new demands, the cries, the anguish that arise around me. Because I am living now and because I am in the breach now. So the parent must include the new as the definition of being a parent at all. Or (as many Cornell parents chose to do) they can exclude the future, declaring flatly that one ideal stands, and must be honored, come what may.

BYERS: The Cornell experience, in the light of the building seizure, is a special example of social crisis, I think. Cornell is an isolated community, unlike Harvard, or Columbia, unlike most of the campuses where disruptions have taken place. Here, no elements foreign to the community could be brought in to obscure the particular issues, and the turmoil the community itself had to undergo. Of course, the issues were broad, they encompassed national and international questions. But the factions in the whole drama were local. Even the parents had a bond with the community, in the sense that they were either Cornell alumni, or had children at Cornell. I think this is one factor that made our drama particularly interesting.

Another factor in the dispute was the faculty and their behavior during the crisis. Would you like to discuss that?

BERRIGAN: I think that with this transition we enter into the heart of the matter. I should perhaps state at the outset that certain convictions arose in me during the crisis that I can now judge at somewhat more distance. And I must say that one conviction remains intact. After attending several faculty meetings during those weeks, I concluded that the faculty would decide the fate of the university. It was quite as simple as that. The mass media, television, the responsible national press, the irresponsible, savage local press, all invariably missed the point. The point was whether or not the faculty, dogged by a history of misuse of power, of stalemate and intrigue and privilege, would rise to the crisis, and choose a new university or no university at all. This was the question.

On Monday, after the building seizure, the faculty refused to reverse themselves on a previous decision to discipline the black students. After a very extended and intense meeting, they stood firm. The blacks were called to account for a few trivial violations of campus order, politically conceived, during the preceding months. By such a decision, blindly or deliberately, the faculty was summoning itself before the bar of the national community and the university. Triviality, egoism, pride (dare one say racism?) were the order of business. Internationally known members of a prestigious community debated and delayed over the issue for hours. Could the university move forward to include new elements of power, a new sharing of power? The faculty answer was a resounding "No." As their decision turned, it was clear that the majority would rather punish a few blacks for a few minor infractions of a few childish rules than to forgive, ignore, adjust, and move forward.

Monday's decision was followed by a wave of anger and frustration. On Tuesday, almost half the student community, some six thousand, seized Barton Hall in support of the blacks. By Wednesday the university was close to a point of no return. We will not soon forget these hours: Lightheaded from a fifty-hour vigil, we waited for the faculty decision as their third major gathering of the week ground on. The mills of the gods? But what contemptible and monor deities!

BYERS: Many of the professors, still worrying the question of academic freedom, changed their votes on Wednesday and gave in to the majority. But their fears and reservations remained. Some of them reverted instinctively to the McCarthy period. Some of them felt that demands for relevant education would kill their particular fields of studies, and make of the university a laboratory for this or that immediate social need. They felt there would be no more room for the perennial long-range aspects of knowledge and research. And while they did change their votes, they felt under duress; they were destroying something in themselves, in the sanctity of the university and in the entire academic community. Could you describe the way you felt toward these reservations, and what you felt Wednesday's faculty vote meant?

BERRIGAN: One way of taking the temperature of the Cornell faculty is to turn to the correspondence page of the New York *Times* in the week or two that followed. Despair, I would think, was the overriding emotion, as the faculty painfully accommodated to the facts of life. The *Times* pointed out editorially that Cornell was the first large prestigious university whose faculty did not quickly line up in support of students demands. Columbia, Harvard, Berkeley, and Wisconsin, when the chips were down, veered around to approve the justice and realism of student demands. Cornell stood firm, almost to the end. This I think was due to the particular situation here; almost half the university faculty is drawn from reactionary schools of law, engineering, history, government, and agriculture, a situation that does not hold on other campuses. So ours was the only "liberal" Ivy League or state university faculty to mount a common front against change. The ramparts were raised and manned, a very Maginot Line of the mind.

Indeed for me, the most depressing experiences of those two weeks was attending faculty meetings and sensing the forces at work there. The older tenured faculty invariably controlled the floor. They made arrangements of convenience with the bureaucracy, as to what questions would arise and what direction the vote would take. It was clear that the large mass of the faculty, after four years of the Vietnam war and two years of rising black consciousness, were unable to read the signs; they were almost entirely devoid of moral conviction and political skills. It made little difference in the outcome of voting that almost all the faculty were in attendance; self-interest remained the only consideration. As a consequence, their debate was invariably elitist, fretful, and blissfully ignorant. They were anxious, as they declared in carefully veiled (and racist) language, to guarantee former arrangement of power, were prepared to lose nothing, determined to yield no jot of power over the university community, over the president, or over their departments or classrooms. Many senior members declared openly that they were quite ready to see the university come down rather than change their vote upon the issues at hand, the punishing of the blacks.

In this regard, I remember an episode in the autumn of 1967, when I arrived at Cornell. President James Perkins declared to me that he had received a letter during the summer signed by some three hundred faculty members, expressing their determination to enter upon some unnamed form of action, if he did not declare immediate war upon student disrupters. The disruptions of that period were mild indeed. Some small number of students sat in at an ROTC review in May of that year. But even at that time, forces of reaction were seriously gathering.

Perkins has now resigned from the university. It is of point, I would think, to recall that the faculty have made good on their threat. His removal was effected by powerful rightist forces determined to make Perkins their scapegoat, powerful enough to bring him down. The replacement of the president by a rightist would, according to this theory, bring the rebels back into line and restore L. and O. Thus far the local intellectual version of the Nixonian theory of social change.

The idea that the removal of the president of Cornell would remove the causes of campus turmoil is as realistic as another idea once commonly held: that the election of a U. S. President in 1968 would remove the causes of national unrest. Indeed, faculty opinions reach far beyond the limits of the university; they have to do with the collision of two theories of history. One theory is armed with every intellectual and military resource possible to a technological, sophisticated society. The other is represented, for the first time, by an incursion into the scene of power of the sons of those in power. And this is a crucial difference in Western culture today, as Eldridge Cleaver understood. The sons of slave masters are joining forces, for the first time, with the sons of slaves. And the outcome, for those determined to keep their slave holdings, is indeed placed in the breach.

B Y E R S : Faced with this new coalition and what it meant to their power, their prestigious roles, their privileged status, the faculty showed itself, I feel, to be a group of fair-weather liberals. Once confronted with crisis, they exposed their real fears, their determination to cling to their prestige, their position, their alliance with "the executioners." They take great pride in disguising all this. But time and again, their real motives came out; what it means to them to be in power (it means literally everything), how hard they are willing to struggle to retain it.

Their tactic was interesting and, in the short run, successful. Consequent on the massive support given the blacks by the university at large (over half the community was involved in the protest seizure of Barton Hall), the reactionary faculty realized at last that they could not successfully prosecute the blacks. So their tactic shifted. The aim now was to force out of office the president of the university, who had been known for his liberal, even courageous stand in defense of certain programs for blacks. A second tactic was to condemn those whites who were most articulate and outspoken in defense of the blacks.

In the days following the seizure of the Straight, the wrath of the faculty against members of SDS and the radical community was increasingly apparent. I believe it was Hans Bethe who said in a meeting that the faculty role must be to isolate the radicals from the majority of the students and then to root them out. In the week following the Straight incident the tactic hardly got anywhere; the faculty simply could not come down between the two groups, black and white. The line against them was also drawn, unexpectedly, by the growing consciousness of the liberals, the "silent center," as they are called. A Concern grew to stand behind the radical movement, black and white, in such a way as to make the Bethe method, in fact, unworkable.

BERRIGAN: Suppose one had held, prior to these weeks, a respectful view of the Cornell faculty as a community dedicated to rational change. Then suppose he were to hear from the floor such opinions as you speak of, uttered by a Nobel Prize winner. Hans Bethe had stood in defense of the values of the mind against a war-making society in the fifties, at a considerable risk to himself. Yet in this year he came forward to denounce the SDS in their efforts to stand with the black community. This I would take to be a bellwether of what was occurring throughout the older faculty ranks. Those forces that had once vindicated the American experience, had welcomed peaceable change and defended civil rights, were now at a stalemate before the demands of a new generation. After years of merciless Vietnam adventuring and years of domestic upheaval, they were standing firm, ultimately with Nixon; law and order must prevail in the university.

The faculty attitude required, of course, an acceptable formula, which they shortly came upon; it was "academic freedom." The slogan was espoused, strangely enough, by those members of the faculty who had been assailed during the McCarthy era. Their intellectual dwellings were filled with skeletons, rattling away in the late sixties, tapping their instructions in a dead language; the expulsion of all who threatened disruption and disunion. It was, once more, the parable of the parents versus the children. Could the parents grow into the lives and hopes of their own sons? Or was the intellectual community, along with the other societal sources of power, stalemated and dried up? Could the faculty legislate only the kind of peace that preserved its own privilege? This was the question. And upon that question the university would either founder or flourish.

Academic freedom! It had been a cry of liberation in the fifties; it became, at least at Cornell, a weapon of suppression in the sixties. Those professors who had once found themselves embattled, without support, threatened in the exercise of free speech, now were using the cry to suppress the demands of students.

I wonder if I could refer here to one professor, who represents a particularly moving example of this turnabout. He was a man of some twenty years' experience on the Cornell faculty. He had innovated a program of studies that had kept reasonably free of government interference. Since the beginning of the Vietnam war, he had even undertaken a scholarly criticism of the military. Yet his was one of the earliest voices of doom raised after the events of mid-May. He warned again and again of the incursion by black and white radicals into academic freedom. I spent several long evenings of discussion with him after the seizure of the Student Union. He remained essentially unchanged in his conviction; freedom to teach at Cornell was being seriously threatened. Another professor, who later resigned, expressed himself in this way: The university has nothing to do with the world! (No one present was so impolitic as to inquire where his research grants were coming from.)

So the days went. Good men closed ranks with adventurers, the blind led the purblind. Stung to righteous anger, prestigious men left the university; others kept silent, hoping the worst would blow over. Very few were willing to face the issues: the sharing of academic power, the pervasive, corrupting military influence upon research and budget, the unexamined, and omnipresent racism. The faculty stood firm, like officers of a sinking ship, both comic and tragic, going down while they saluted the invisible gods "who demand such things." Might they, and their ship, be saved? To many, the question did not refer. Something called freedom was worth it all: the ship, the lives. Many seemed unable to realize that the sharing of academic power was in fact an opportunity for them to lift their lives out of the rut of irrelevant research, misspent public moneys, and utter indifference toward students. Too much to ask! A specter was conjured up, a common nightmare; it showed the faculty, denuded of laurels and rewards, assailed from the left by forces of disorder and disruption and anti-intellectualism.

Indeed, how does a university professor come to realize that at this point of history, after resistance to the draft, after life in the ghetto, white and black students alike are the true victims of academic unfreedom? To the blacks and the SDS, the phrase, "academic freedom" as used at Cornell in 1969, symbolizes one thing only; the reduction of students to a nigger or ghetto level of silence and submission. The good student, like the good nigger, knows his place. The truth comes to him from on high, he traffics in indulgences, and if he is assiduous and lucky, he gains an entrance (of sorts) into the system.

BYERS: Is it any wonder that the students subjected to the "truth from on high" method, view academic freedom with a certain reserve? They know how great a price is paid for this so-called privilege. They know that the university has a large stake in one side of the issues, one side presented as though it were the only side. This is why the movement questions the talk about academic freedom. Why do professors feel that the SDS, black liberation movements, the Third World Liberation Front, the resistance are such threats to their freedom? Their freedom has already been sold. It was bartered for money to carry on research in their fields, at the will of the government. Some 23.5 million dollars of Cornell's 40 million dollars of annual research is carried on for the benefit of the government; much of the research is for military and paramilitary purposes. It would seem to us who live with the facts and even dream of bringing about real change that this is too great a price to pay for purported academic freedom.

BERRIGAN: I remember hearing, on many occasions during these weeks, declarations by faculty members to the effect that the university must, by its very nature, in accord with the function it performs, be kept apart from society. I think this is another way of getting at the extremely complex issue of academic freedom. Whose freedom is at stake? And could it not be that one form of freedom is guarded only at the price of the enslavement of others? A certain humility is called for here. Such humility would, ideally, govern a professor's conduct not merely toward his students, toward the forms of research he chooses to undertake. It would also govern his attitude toward the university as such. Indeed, is the university, as presently governed, beyond serious criticism? In any sane view it must be considered open to the most serious reservations of thoughtful men. A large topic indeed.

II

But the development of the topic would go something like this. The university, as presently conducted, is a function of technological American society. The university does not exist to analyze, interpret, or gainsay the self-understanding of the culture it serves. It has no prophetic gift or function. It is in no sense "over against" its culture. Given the alignment between university and society, to which the president of Cornell often paid tribute, it would seem to follow that no professor can declare himself immune, within whatever ivory tower, from the tribute demanded of him by his society. The fact is that from the classics to the arts (and much more obviously within the pure and applied sciences and the social sciences), the university must pay up; it depends in a pragmatic, hard-cash way upon the government for its survival. No university, whether private or public, can exist for a single year without a massive income derived directly from the federal government and aimed directly at the furtherance of federal purposes; that is to say, in many cases, paramilitary or overt military purposes. The ivory tower is not only crumbling; it is being rapidly dismantled. And no student or professor can feel secure from danger to his career and security as long as his survival, research, and prestige depend on forces that by and large, lie beyond his control.

Solid evidence would suggest then that the survival of the university, as we have known it, cannot much longer depend upon the faculty. We at Cornell have seen firsthand their ability to deal with crisis. Their view of human knowledge and society and the human person is platonic almost beyond cure. Moreover, their rhetoric about themselves is laden with egoism and self-protection and fear of human change. Maybe we are holding a kind of death service over the university as we have known it. Maybe our real task is to begin discussing aspects of freedom that might survive it.

I must state at this point my conviction that if Cornell does not survive, its destruction will have very little to do with SDS or the blacks. They are merely unmasking the real forces at work. The demise of Cornell will almost certainly have to be laid at the door of the faculty itself. It is not the black occupation of the Student Union that provokes our question. It is the coalition of labyrinthine politics and faculty folly, mounting in sum to a very Everest of foolishness, moral immobility, and duplicity, which make the question a pointed and even a poignant one. But one could go deeper. Given the neglected and historically violated priorities that America has forced down the starving jaws of the world (as her trade brand of truth and nourishment), the question inevitably arises whether or not Cornell *deserves* to survive.

This indeed may be a closer approximation to the real question facing us. The question of creeping ivy upon venerable walls in the year of our Lord 1969, the year of Nixon's will, the year

of black fury and white, the year of despair in cities, the year
when butter is again denied the hungry and their bodies are
detonated instead with iron explosives—this is the year in which
one must ask himself how much sentiment we can afford when
our struggle is reduced to one of simple survival. At what point,
pushed against the wall for how long, must the heart harden
itself, as a sign that it rightly occupies the breast of man, an
organ of understanding, clairvoyance, passion? How much ivy
indeed can we afford, when the ivy is poisoned? The defoliants
sprayed upon that ivy are the very acid of human anger, loosed
upon our institutions as a consequence of willful and foolish
power, tinkering with the precarious enterprise of human history
itself.

When one episode, necessarily fragmented and clumsy and
localized, is attuned to real history, everything fits together. That
is to say, the Cornell experience, brief and mindless as it was in
many aspects, is still parabolic. Cornell is our society. As those
who know something of our history can attest, Cornell includes
both the best and the worst of America under one honorable
roof. The best; it has nurtured in the last years both whites and
blacks who are determined, beyond the threat of death, to achieve
a measure of decency that will justify their existence. That generation of students, born in the furnaces of Vietnam resistance
and of the ghetto, finds itself assailed by the powers that claim
authority over them, in public, and increasingly in private.

The blacks! They were first welcomed to Cornell as a kind of
surgical measure—the removal of a stigma from the white body.
In 1965 the first group to be accountable in any real sense for
their own future arrived in Ithaca. They numbered thirty-nine
in a community of some fourteen thousand; they were largely
drawn, as were those who followed, from poor urban areas.

What was expected of them was entirely predictable, from the
point of view of the white establishment. That is to say, they
were to show by public and private demeanor, by their "performance" (in the manner of untrained animals), a will to get
ahead, to advance to the center ring of the white man's circus.

At the end of four years' bartering they would emerge into society, bearing a first-class (almost) ticket of admission. The plan was admirable, as a plan. The trouble was that in the event it simply did not go far enough. It did not reckon with the forces that the society itself had unleased: war, racist backlash, violence, political and economic repression. Campus arrangements were altered overnight. The blacks who were brought to Cornell in the rear seats of white conveyances simply decided not to pay for the trip. They underwent a mysterious change in the act of opening their books, in the act of meeting their brothers from the internal colonies, in the act of comparing notes with the wretched of the earth. Education! It was intoxicating, it spelled trouble.

The trouble was two cents plain. They began to ask unpleasant questions. What was it to be black in a racist circus? What sort of future might blacks expect? What was a human being today, anyway? All hell was loosened, against all expectation, in the simple process of handing the slave boy a primer. For the fact was that blacks now had in hand the tools they needed to evaluate, close up, the forces operative in the society. In the act of accepting the ticket of admission, they rejected the process of admission. And the end of their education was by no means the gentlemen's agreement which the gentlemen had so deliberately arranged. They were not at Cornell to ape the white ethos of violence, imperialism, and domestic control. They were in the university simply to learn to assemble a time bomb. "Look out Whitey, black power's goin' get your mama!" It was not entirely by chance; as Julius Lester acknowledges, the phrase was a borrowed one; it was coined at Cornell.

It was an ironic folk commentary, a warning in black patois, of the forces that were gathering. It says, Watch out; you cannot place books in the hands of the victim without setting in motion forces that the slave master cannot long dictate or control. This was simply a fact of life, a fact of history, a fact of the inevitable turnabout in the distribution of power. Suppose an enlightened decision at Cornell; the poor blacks are admitted in numbers, a repressive majority decides to liberalize its policy.

Really on its mind is a strangle hold on the future; "Admit the black leaders, educate them, cajole them, whitewash them." But the tactic fails. It fails as I saw in South Africa four years ago, and at Cornell within the past year. Nothing finally avails against history except extermination. And for that, on the domestic scene at least, American men of power are not quite ready. They are not ready for it, let us say without cynicism, not because they are men of conscience, or men for whom the placing of limits upon death is a postulate of compassion. They are not ready for the tactic because it is not yet "publicly admissible." It will not do to localize the Vietnam method (in spite of the helicopter seeding students and faculty at Berkeley with tear gas). Maybe soon, but not quite yet. Unlimited violence at a distance, exercised against the gooks, is entirely admissible. But at home, the middle class is not yet resigned to losing its sons as the price of keeping its property. And until this scruple is resolved, a certain limitation of violence against "fellow Ammurricans" is necessarily in force.

The second fact to be dealt with is the creation of a new generation of white American youth as a result of the war. I remember, in this regard, being invited some time ago to share a television platform in Chicago with General Hershey. I debated with myself on the airplane, approaching the Great Lakes, how best to communicate to this iron-bound gentleman my sense of his contribution to the national scene. I resolved that I would congratulate him for a simple and momentous achievement. It seemed to me that he had helped younger America pass into an entirely new phase of spiritual development. In place of the frivolity and childishness of the campus scene in the forties and fifties, we now had youths seriously intent upon resistance and dissent against the American death scene. And this was no mean achievement, to have helped a whole generation come on a new way. It argued to the creation of new men, a kind of leap in existence. General Hershey had done it; no more panty raids on campus. On to the barricades! Burn your draft card!

My dream (every American boy dreams of meeting General

H.) was disrupted by his decision not to enter into debate with me at all. The general had evidently not been told that he was to face the camera with a convicted felon; not any felon at all, but a hit-and-stand raider of his preserve. The general is an old-line public servant, a witness, of sorts, to conscience of sorts. He stalked off the stage, not about to share tube time with a man who had set fires going in his deer park.

But the achievement remains, and should at least be recorded, in however fumbling a way. The general and the Presidents he served, from Kennedy through Johnson and Nixon, have brought entirely new moral forces into being. (That is to say, one man's nightmare is another man's vision.) America now has within its precincts, a great wooden horse, rolled in against all expectation, pregnant with our future and our doom. On some night, at Cornell, at the Pentagon, in the inner black ghetto, a genetic miracle occurred. The wooden animal came to birth. The horse disgorged its armies of fury, to overturn the law and order that some men rightly discerned was nothing more than lawlessness and disorder. The armies overran the city, leaving in their wake dismay and destruction.

"Black and white together"; the old freedom lyrics, with all their sentimental acumen, took a new turn. With jail, the threat of cops, and the shared hatred of the establishment, a new beginning was under way. A common fate was born, governed by a communal tactic. The SDS at Cornell was not slow to recognize that the action of their black brothers had opened a way for them also. The cup was passed; an intoxicating moment of liberation. All during that Saturday, into Sunday's dawn, the blacks saw from within the occupied building an extraordinary sight; hundreds of white brothers were standing outside in the cold, protecting the illegal occupants of Willard Straight from jocks and cops. It was, as Eldridge Cleaver earlier realized, a moment of supreme irony. Blacks and whites, if only for a moment, had come together in a common purpose. A future worthy of man was being prepared by both sides.

The old authority was bankrupt. It could speak for neither

side. The whites spiritually stood within the occupied building, the blacks spiritually ringed the building. And even though a common language had yet to be forged, and many differences and misunderstandings were yet to be ironed out, both sides were conscious that something unprecedented had occurred; hands had reached out in the darkness, touched, tightened, one within the other. "A terrible beauty is born."

And something else came home to me. Catonsville, I exulted in the cold, had reached beyond itself. I now understood, as I was certain that the blacks within the building understood, that in resisting war-making America, we stood with them and they with us. It was a triumph that took nothing from the triumph of one's brothers.

For the president of Cornell, these days bore a far different import. Dr. Perkins had every reason to believe that his university status was secure. He had been one of the first across the country to sense the direction of things. He had initiated a black studies program and had been hailed dutifully in the pages of the New York *Times*. So he had every reason to believe that the blacks would respond gratefully, once their goals, as he perceived them, were peaceably won. Alas and alas, Mr. Perkins is the prime example of a historic fact; that the fact composes his obituary at Cornell is also instructive. The point is, as his meteoric fall illustrates, that liberalism is simply not good enough. Dr. Perkins (a Quaker of roughly the same level of spiritual perception as Mr. Nixon) found nothing anomalous in the larger honors he had assumed beyond the campus. He sat gracefully upon the board of Chase Manhattan and the board of the United Negro College Fund. He could pay lip service at home to the black cause or the issues raised by SDS; he could declare something else at some distance, as he did in Boston at a meeting of Cornell alumni in the spring of 1969. The Ivy League would be well advised, he said on that occasion, to stand by its brother, Father Theodore Hesburgh of Notre Dame. That distinguished cleric will be remembered as the first of the big stick boys. He also

introduced the stopwatch onto the campus scene; fifteen minutes
to go, then call the cops.

It may not be entirely charitable, it is merely an example of
the iron march of history, to note that these dizzying heights
of moral compromise were ultimately too much for Dr. Perkins.
His dream collapsed, and he with it. This is not to refuse tribute
to his considerable skill in assaying the risks, in resolving to dare
them. Could the president of Cornell authorize anti-insurgency
operations, contracted for with the government, at the Aeronautical Laboratory at Buffalo, and at the same time seriously welcome black students to his campus? Could he make peace at
home and prepare for war in Buffalo? Could he both butter and
bomb? If he could, perhaps the liberal style, in spite of all stresses
and threats, could make it.

It could not. The president had arranged a symposium on
South Africa, a delaying tactic against SDS demands for inves-
tigation of university investments in that apartheid state. He
arose to speak at the final session; his words enraged a portion
of his hearers, and he was physically set upon by a black student.
It is of small moment that the sum of damage done to his person
was a rumpling of his jacket. The point was, as both sides recognized with a start (either of recognition or of horror), that a
moment had been reached. The moment was variously feared,
dreaded, passionately desired. But its impact was clear. The president was no longer inviolate against the forces he had helped set
in motion. His well-being could never again depend upon
aesthetic distance—from the facts of violence in the ghetto, or of
violence in Vietnam. His career was as expendable as the lives of
distant insurgents against whom the Aeronautical Laboratory was
ranging the university on its Buffalo properties. The ghetto
swarmed into the playground; the playground was condemned.
Dr. Perkins had passed, in the classical sense of Blake, from
innocence to experience.

Imagine! A black student who three or four years earlier had
been admitted to Cornell under supposition that he would keep
the park rules, respect the park equipment, keep off the grass,

depart peaceably at dusk—this man suddenly broke all the rules. More, he held the rules up to ridicule; they had been written by children for children. In the case of men, they simply did not signify. What did it all mean? Was the playground in fact bought, maintained, patrolled by the sweat and tears of those who mowed its lawns, hewed its wood, and drew its water? Was the black resisting a role that had been meticulously created for him—to join the keepers and owners at the expense of those upon whose backs lay the real burdens of privilege? Had some miraculous arc been joined in his consciousness? Did he sense a connection between the good life he was enjoying through Cornell investments and the slave labor of his South African brothers?

His intuition was right; it was in accord with the truth. By laying hands on the president of the university, in an obvious and shocking breach of good manners or civilized conduct, he was expressing the outrage and impatience of the semiliberated, for whom the timepieces of the powerful never move quickly enough.

Slowly, with killing slowness, grind the mills of the great. Never fast enough. I questioned a black student earlier this year: "Is the tactic, then, to push a little and gain a little; then to push hard and gain a great deal?" He looked at me, and slowly shook his head. "No, man; like this: Push with everything you've got, and gain practically nothing!"

So in the society, so at Cornell. Whether he was seeking medical aid, justice, dialogue with professors, economic equity, respect from white students, or indeed the support of the religious establishment, a black student shortly realized the massive opposition to change that hemmed him in.

After the seizure of the Student Union, many of us moved about the campus, trying to interpret events with students for whom the events were literally beyond grasp. How could one learn to read in the course of a single week, when his life had prepared him only for a kind of spiritual illiteracy? How could he learn to read as he ran, when events were running so fast? I was invited into the Veterinary School to speak to faculty and students. In the course of that afternoon I suggested that the school set up a series of seminars to acquaint faculty and students with the issues implicit in the seizure of the campus building. So it came about, for the first time (as far as anyone knew) in the history of the vet school, that black students appeared before veterinary students to explain the seizure of a campus building, and to discuss its implications for the whole campus. The black students were at pains to make clear that their demands embraced the community they had come from, as well as the community to which they were returning. They were seeking the establishment of a Cornell college in Harlem. They were working in the black community of Ithaca, long exploited and controlled by the economics of the university.

Such a degree of understanding was of course unprecedented; it left the run-of-the-mill white student quite unable to cope or compare. Could white students at Cornell grasp the connection between assuming a measure of control over their lives and liberation of the poor (presuming the students had any conception of the fate of minorities within their society)? The black intuition was both simple and staggering. Justice for one meant justice for all. A decent environment for one, or for a few, meant that decency must be restored or created for all. The rebellion of blacks at Cornell must in the nature of things illumine the fact that nonwhite peoples around the world were being exploited and destroyed by a common method. To that method must correspond a common reaction, based upon a common ethos and consciousness.

To be a black at Cornell, that is, could not be a different thing from being a black in the gold mines of Johannesburg, or a Congolese at the mercy of white man's guns, or a Venezuelan oil worker cursed with the vocation to enrich the Rockefellers. Being judged by the system of Cornell could not be a different thing than being dealt with by the judicial system in New York City, or a *favellista* in Rio, or a Viet Cong in Saigon. It was all one, it was a common destiny legislated by a universal overseer.

To have a cross burned on the lawn of a black cooperative

at Cornell could not be separated from the fate of Edmund Till, his broken body cast into the waters of the Mississippi River. The blacks saw this, and they acted. One might, if he wished to wax lyrical, celebrate a leap in consciousness. Or he might simply say that the black man had learned to put his head together. Subject belongs with predicate, and both with object. And where the object in white minds is violence, the logic of subject and predicate dictate that action be taken on behalf of victims here, there, and everywhere. Wherever that is, a black or brown or yellow or red man determines in whatever tentative or non-violent way to be simply a man. Such a man must be supported by his brothers. That was the issue, raised by a single provocation.

And the provocation simply could not be borne with. That went without saying. A black must be content to be less than a man, as the price of survival at all. Or if he determined to survive as a man, he must undergo risk to his life, he must face the threat of extinction.

The president of Cornell might refer to the cross-burning incident as a "weekend caper," as he referred to Vietnam as "tedious," as he attempted to gloss over the war research of the Aeronautical Laboratory and attempted to justify university investments in South Africa. Black consciousness was clenched in a fist. It would come down upon the brain pan with a wounding blow. It would prefer one kind of violence to the total violence of the rotting intellect, pleading in its demise for something called civilized discourse and dialogue.

What was that intellect really seeking, in the president and faculty and trustees, during what might be the last days of empire? It was hegemony, control, power of life and death over men who struggled for a rational sharing of power, for the nonviolent solution of human difference. Sharing of power? That, given the history of these United States, culminating in the history of Vietnam and of the ghettos, was simply intolerable. Liberalism was skilled and enormously powerful in its method; it could weaken beyond all recognition the native clarity of the real question: Could men live together, share their power, form communities based on mutual respect, renounce violence and exploitation as social methods? Or must they choose violence and duel to the death?

Liberalism was not good enough. President Perkins resigned.

One could have wished, when Robert McNamara or Arthur Goldberg stepped off the scene, for some public utterance. Why could such men no longer support the policies of their government? After an iniquitous situation has run its course, another war, another "generation" of weapons, another decade of neglect and destruction, the best the liberals can manage is a tardy, utterly useless statement by some Clark Clifford or other. The chickens, in the unbearable words of Malcolm X, were coming home to roost. The homing instinct, the revenge of outraged history. The liberal response is predictable: Too little and too late. Too little to save even the liberals, too late perhaps to save the liberal society. Dr. Perkins departed.

The faculty and trustees had indeed removed the albatross from about their neck, and tossed it overboard; a liberation of sorts. But had anything really happened, beyond the emptiest of symbolic gestures? The mariner had freed himself, in a manner of speaking, from any inhibition against fishing freely in poisoned waters. But the issues raised by the blacks remained to haunt the powers at Cornell. If the truth were told, to change the president of the university was as empty as the changing of a palace guard—or the changing of American Presidents. From Kennedy to Johnson to Nixon: change of venue, persistence of method. And likewise at Cornell. Whatever new president should be inducted, swearing whatever oaths, to uphold whatever dignity and tradition, the old game would be enforced and the same rules applied.

This is only to suggest that a good man in any position is powerless if his power is rendered void by others. What difference indeed occurred in method, if national rhetoric passed from "military advisers" to the fact of five hundred thousand American troops on Southeast Asian soil? What difference would it make at Cornell, if a new president, announcing this or that change of method or procedure, were nonetheless caught between the upper and lower millstones of trustees and faculty? Power was determined in its course and would not be shaken. Whatever figurehead was carved and placed at the prow, the direction of the voyage would remain unchanged.

President Perkins had written (in *The University in Transition*):

"Universities and other institutions of society—including the corporation, the farm, the cultural center, and the government agency—had now been joined together by a new kind of blood stream, made up of the ideas, the trained intelligence, and the manpower which provide the driving energy for our society. And the University is the great pumping heart that keeps this system fresh, invigorated, and in motion."

Indeed. Dr. Perkins might go under, but the ethos for which he spoke, on behalf of which he saw himself and the university as indispensable, could not so easily be shaken. Obviously, the university was organic to the national body, one of its noblest parts. But indispensable? Only to a degree. The university might remain free in measure, to carry forward a tradition of good sense, respect for intelligence, some resistance against political uniformity and militarism. It granted sanctuary to dissenters; in the long, open season declared by the military, that was important —for the hunted.

But the political aims of the Republic granted no such ground. Its fist was aimed at the groin of the dissenter. America had cops, it had armies, it had nuclear installations and laboratories, it had Mace and tear gas and helicopters. All those resources, all those men and machines, had been tested over a long period, from domestic proving grounds to Panamanian encounters, and on through Vietnam. It was not to be thought that because the university would show some measure of understanding, some breadth of insight, the Republic would honor the same rules of combat. No, America was not about to lose face, it was not about to go under. The university might be concerned with the nuances and feints and shadow play of the intellect in crisis;

but the gut game of politics and the military had other, quicker methods at hand. The United States was no Hamlet, sequestered on remote acres, muttering immortal inanities to itself. No, the way to "keep what we have" was to wage war for it. Johnson said so; he ought to know. And that was the graffiti scrawled upon the walls of Saigon, as upon the walls of the ghetto. "We keep what we have. Gooks and niggers, take notice."

The faculty, moving in strongly from the right, demanded and won the resignation of Dr. Perkins. The Board of Trustees completed the ying-yang. These latter gentlemen, of known power and virtue, deserve some measure of scrutiny.

Perhaps the main interest group in the Cornell trusteeship lies with the Rockefeller domain. The controllers of Standard Oil of New Jersey, of American Express, the Rockefeller Foundation, of Chase Manhattan, of Eastern Airlines, of Sunoco Mobil Oil, of the Metropolitan Life Insurance Company and the Equitable Life Assurance Society have not been remiss in their interests on the Ithaca campus. In 1968, Robert Purcell was elected chairman of the board of the Cornell trustees. His main connection with the Rockefeller interests is his chairmanship of the board of the International Basic Economy Corporation. IBEC was founded in 1947 by Nelson Rockefeller "to meet the crying need for modernization in Latin America at the end of World War II." He saw it as "an economic development corporation for fomenting and energizing business, to increase the production and availability of goods and services basic to the lives of people in less developed countries." Beyond the jargon lies the tactic: Leviathan need move in only one of his parts, and the whole sea is altered.

Most United States firms, of course, were involved, long before IBEC, in extracting resources from the Third World, seizing upon primary products, to be processed in the technologically developed countries. But IBEC was more subtle in its method. It introduced into Latin America a measure of indigenous development; built supermarkets; processed milk; produced poultry; constructed housing; served as a source of mutual funds and investments. It entered the Third World and shouldered aside, with its more sophisticated methods, those reserves usually left by mutual agreement to the indigenous power elites.

A look at Venezuela, favorite territory for Rockefeller modernizers, points out the success of the dynasty in creating new forms of foreign control. Venezuela's main wealth lies in oil deposits. Each year she ships three billion dollars' worth of oil into foreign markets. Rockefeller's Creole Petroleum Corporation controls more than 40 percent of the total production and sales volume of oil; Gulf, Mobil, and Shell together account for most of the remainder of Venezuelan oil resources. (The Venezuelan government-owned groups have "concessionary rights," less than 1 percent of the Venezuelan reserve.) Harvey O'Conner tells of the results of such benign trusteeship: "Before the discovery and exploitation of oil reserves, Venezuela fed itself somehow. Today it produces only one-half the corn, one-half the meat, one-third the green vegetables and grains, and one-half the milk it consumes. There are fewer cattle than at the time of the revolution of 1812." Yet, the Rockefeller entrepreneurs and other foreign interests can point to a celebrated fact: Today Venezuela is in a better economic condition than any other Latin American country. She has the highest per capita income on the continent, some eight hundred dollars per annum.

Two years after James Perkins accepted the presidency of Cornell, the Rockefellers funded the Cornell Latin American Year. Opening speeches were delivered by Dr. Perkins and by J. George Harrar, President of the Rockefeller Foundation. They outlined the purpose of the year; to draw international attention to the university's Latin American Studies Program. Soon after the Rockefeller-Latin American celebration had finished its ritual of seminars, visiting experts, and lecturers, Dr. Perkins was invited (the only president of an American university so honored) to sit with the directors of Chase Manhattan Bank, the primary financial interest of the Rockefeller empire.

A link between Cornell and the fate of the South African

nonwhite peoples was hereby forged. So, as it turned, a link was joined in the chain of events that was to destroy the Cornell phase of Perkins' career. Following the Sharpeville Massacre, foreign investors began to withdraw from the South African economy, fearing a takeover by the blacks. To end this crisis and protect investments, Chase Manhattan, together with ten other major U.S. banks, entered a consortium, offering extended credit loans to the South African government. During the same period, Chase sought and obtained additional U.S. capital for South African investments. Shored up by credit loans for banking consortia, and the speedy re-entry of foreign investment under the aegis of Chase Manhattan, the South African government effectively put down the liberation movement within its borders. The rewards have been enormous. Chase Manhattan is now the eighth largest bank in South Africa. Its policy of going where the money is has paid off handsomely. (Thus in 1966 it was able to announce that "in Saigon too, you have a friend at Chase Manhattan.")

In 1967, Governor Nelson Rockefeller appointed Harold Uris to the Cornell board of trustees. The Uris interests were already joined with those of the Rockefellers on the real estate scene of New York City. A complicated series of deals there enabled Uris Brothers to undercut the Zeckendorf interests. The Uris Corporation finally announced, in 1969, a joint building venture, involving their company and Rockefeller Center, for the raising of a skyscraper office building in Manhattan at Fifty-first Street and the Avenue of the Americas.

Another powerful family interest is that of the Olins, represented on the Cornell campus by gifts of chemistry and physics buildings, and the enormous Olin Graduate Library, one of the largest in the world. Olin of course relies heavily on government purchases for military, space, and foreign "aid." The 12-gauge shotgun produced by the Winchester Western Division of the Olin-Mathieson Corporation is also a basic antiriot weapon of several metropolitan police departments.

The Johnsons of Johnson's Wax represent another style in the agglomerate of Cornell University interests. The Johnsons are a cultural force here and abroad. They are Trustees of the International Chamber of Commerce and sit on the National Industrial Conference Board and the Committee for Economic Development. Their contribution to Cornell is mainly in artistic directions: They have donated some four million dollars for the building of a new art museum. (They have also set up foundations for the study of domestic social problems, arms control, and poverty.) But the Johnsons' interests move in other directions as well. One of the family, Samuel C., is a director of Cutler-Hammer, a producer of electronic and reconnaissance systems for the Department of Defense. Johnson and Son is also in the forefront of military and economic expansion abroad. By 1970, foreign sales will reach some 50 percent of the total volume of their production, mainly in the areas of electronic reconnaissance systems for the Department of Defense. The RAND Corporation and the Institute for Defense Analysis pay tribute to the groundwork laid by the Johnsons; they are studying means of applying Cutler-Hammer reconnaissance systems to urban areas in the United States. Black revolutionaries and white resisters, take notice.

And so on. It would be tedious to explore Cornell's foreign policy establishment, its link with the defense nexus, its connection, through its former president, through Walter Cizler, through the Deans, John Collyer, Nicholas Noyes, William Carey, and others, with apartheid in South Africa. This last issue remains a grievous one on campus. The Cornell SDS began in the spring of 1968 to campaign for the sale of Cornell University stocks held in banks which invest in nonwhite misery in southern Africa. The campaign garnered a single trustee vote for divesting of such funds. The response makes the only kind of sense one can expect of "cash and carry" ethics. Eleven Cornell trustees are directors of firms that have investments in South Africa. The challenge to Cornell is, of course, by strong implication, a threat to their own investments. Moreover, even for trustees whose firms are not directly involved in South African horrors, the idea that human welfare should supersede the profit motive as a guide for foreign investment is simply absurd. Moreover, such a question inevitably risks opening the messy box of other investments in other areas of the world also controlled by racists and dominated by outsiders.

The SDS lost, temporarily. But a short time later, sensing the winds, Cornell quietly divested itself of South African investments. And within six months, Dr. Perkins resigned. Indeed, the shadow of South Africa lies like a plague on the enchanted playground. There is very little fun these days in the Fun House. "Co'nell and Ha'vard done ruined mo' good niggers 'an liquor anyday." So spoke the black changeling, Junebug J. Jones.

Can we make it without bloodshed? The question applies to Black Panthers, Angola guerrillas, Camilo Torres, the Viet Cong, and other otherwise nice people like the Cornell community (not to mention the United States Army). The same Junebug, speaking at Cornell the day after the occupation of the Straight, on May 4, put it like it is. (His words echo those of another seer, whose sayings have gotten about.) What he said went to the point; gun barrels raised there and then against the Omnipotent Owners, guns produced, traded, bought, sold, hoarded, dreaded, lusted after by trustees, faculty, and students, by all of us otherwise nice people. "All sho'nuff dialogue comes from the barrel of a gun." Indeed.

Epilogue

One

PAUPERES SEMPER:
A NONENCYCLICAL

There was once a Good Man who used to address Words of
Wisdom to all the people. He told the Rich to loosen up on
their Bank Reserves, Government People to get going on Social
Services, and the Military to control the Passion for New Hard-
ware. He expressed the Feeling that if Children were around,
there should be Schools, and that if people were ill, hospitals
ought to be Available; he said that no one ought to Starve, or
to sleep in the open Weather, which was severe in most places.

When Brush Wars broke out in remote Provinces he sat up
most of the Night, worrying and poring over Letters to both
sides, urging the Leaders to Cool It and the Other Tribes not
to add Fuel to the Fire.

This Activity got him into trouble sometimes. Influential People read his Writings (even though they had their own Holy
Men), mainly because it was the Thing to Do. The Rich saw that
they were mentioned; they were Not Pleased. They fumed about
Industry and Austerity, the Blessings of Unfettered Free Enterprise, and insisted that they were pulling More than their Load,
that they had worked since the Third Hour, that they were bearing the Heat of the Day alone. They also hinted strongly that it
would be much better if Certain Priests would stay in the Sacristy,
from which (on their Knees) they might see Things in Better
Perspective.

The Military took a stance of Injured Dignity. Was not the

Worth of their Activity Self-Evident? They went right on with their Seven-Day Work Week, serving the People. They had a cave in the hills run by a World Combine, Vulcane-Marse, Ltd. High Security prevailed; the sound of trip hammers could be heard in the surrounding countryside All Day, and the Hissing of Steam and Smoke from the Blast Furnaces. Air Pollution was grievous, but the Government published a study showing that the families of the Area had a remarkably high Inner Personal Security Ratio.

It was announced that the Military were working on weapons that would, once and for All, Secure Our Boundaries from Aggression.

When asked to comment on the Good Man's words referring to "a Senseless Arms Race," and "Neglect of the Deeper Needs of Society," a Public Relations Man responded with a virtuous Blank Stare. He said that Mr. Vulcane, of High Ordinance Anti-Personnel Research, would be Unavailable for comment; General Marse also was absent; he was leading an Escalation Scenario Session up the River. But both Leaders had agreed on a Statement. National Security Forbade them to say much; they were confident, however, without descending to the Particulars of An Attack which must seem, in View of the Uneasy International Climate, highly Regrettable, that the Good Sense of the Electorate, and eventually, History Itself, would vindicate the Wisdom of Their Course. Mr. Bonzane of Military P.R. would now endeavor to answer any questions.

Yes, military expenditures were *somewhat* above last year's.

No, Absolutely no. There was no correlation between the facts of domestic poverty, and this necessary, and modest military increase. The poorer classes, who were also gifted with good sense, would appreciate this, and join cheerfully in the National Sacrifice.

No. He could be definitive on this one; no further military increase was anticipated In Our Time. Positively Not.

No Detailed Accounting could be Given of the Allocation of the Military Budget. In view of National Security; Of Course Not. But the People could be assured that as always, Austerity governed the Judgment of Those Responsible. A Full Bang for every Buck, if he might be allowed to be facetious.

Well, that was that. A predictable outcome once more. Everyone read the words of the Good Man; they came by the Thousands to hear Him talk on his tours. Then they went back and lived pretty much as they had before.

When he spoke at the Town Hall, they made sure the Stock Exchange was closed for the afternoon; and the Military always switched their combine to Partial Production for the duration of His Stay. But once He had left, everything Hottened up Again. The Rich went on finding Spectacular ways of making more and more Money. The Military announced with a Straight Face that sixty-eight separate Improvements were needed on Last Year's Ultimate Weapons, if our borders were not to be Overrun, once and for all.

The Poor also went back to the Same Old Life. They were herded about, Watched by the Police, prodded and probed by Social Scientists, overcharged, overcrowded, displaced by another City Hall Renovation-of-Neighborhoods Plan, extorted and exhorted, urged to Patience With Their Lot, accused of not observing the Guidelines for Child Limitation. Alas. The Holy Man seemed to be on their side, but he lived far away, and one visit in a lifetime to their Developing Sector didn't seem to solve much, one way or another.

Normalcy, that's the great National Need, said the new president of the International Association of Laissez-Faire. Normal times. Get the chicken back into the dinner pail.

Security, declared the Chief of Staff. That's our business, positively. And we mean to deliver. Just one more push on weaponry research, and no foreign boot will ever desecrate our soil.

Normal and secure, part of the normal scene, secure in the consolations of scripture, the poor went on living in their preserves and *favellas* and bidonvilles and ghettos and inner cities, their work camps and shanty towns. They slept soundly, their psyches blessed with the historic promise: They would always be with us. Indeed, anyone with half an eye could see; they had chosen the Better Part.

Two

HUNGER

There was once a people composed of spare parts and debris, who had evolved into mega-intelligence. Their bodies also had perfectly adapted to the landscape of the postcataclysmic era. They swung and lurched along quite handily in the pits and ruts of the land, stirring up, the while, choking clouds of dust, which they promptly sucked into their tubular system, converting the foulest of matter into vapor, lubricants, and even enzymes.

This people were of an unsurpassed variety and function. They were named, now quaintly, now with irony, according to the strong or weak points in the nature of each.

Thus, Lunar Lander was flat-soled and insect in form. He was equipped, moreover, with a drill snout that dug, like a pig after truffles, for the austere tidbits afforded by the times—glass, stones, sticks, quartzes, bones.

Artful Dodger was skilled in stripping small equipment from others; he stole in close, neutralized their sonar, and made off with the nuts and bolts and small indispensables that kept the hominoids in working order.

Dispos-All was saw-toothed, saw-armed, saw-toed, a killer. He crept about sideways, on four crab feet that bit at the dust spitefully and raked it into a finer dust. Every inch of his surface was offensive and lethal. His midsection opened like a shark's jaw, his proper mouth was an arsenal. His eyes were pincers. There was no waste on him, nothing for pleasure. Where the private parts are, even in superhumanoids, he had an immense magnetized rod; it shot out quicker than thought, made contact, and pulled the victim bodily into striking distance.

Thrasher was a workhorse, a metal beast who carried on his back a tin owner; or in troika, Thrashers bore about their affluent homonoid masters in a sledge. He was skinny and ill-tempered and seemed to have fallen forward, by failure of a ramrod backbone, from some former higher two-footed estate. A rare example of technological regression.

The people dwelt in sheet metal boxes, underground. They communicated, it was said, without words, were generally nervy and humorless, mistrusted one another, and fought frequently to the death. Some of them lasted, but for violence, all but forever.

But if one thing made them memorable, it was surely their hunger. This people were voracious as metal locusts on the loose after metal harvests. They ate everything in sight, and when that was gone—there never was much—they turned with a clumsy, disoriented fury to devouring one another.

They rooted up coal, pig iron, tin, manganese, copper. They came on fossils, old ivory, and curved bone, and ground them up in a moment. Now and again, they came on springs of oil. The discovery, by rumor or odor, charged them with frenzy. They came groaning, clanking, rasping, screeching, a lunar nightmare. When the drill had struck, they drank oil, sloshed in oil, laid down in it, pissed in it, sat on it, fought and killed for it. Intoxicating! Then the geysers dried up again, the black earth turned to dust like everything else and blew away. When there was no more oil, they dreamed of oil. The fathers scooped up dust and poured it on the heads of children. Oil, they said; it was once like that. But the children, grown up if they were lucky, had no such memories. They turned bestial and ate their own children.

Sex dried up too. Machine on machine, the love play became murderous. They fell over in a frenzy, one atop the other. They thrashed there like turtles, easy prey to the marauders who were always abroad. That was how love ended; one no longer dared such a combat, one could too easily be crushed or dismembered where he lay.

But their hunger! Everything came down to that, it was all the meaning of their lives. No one could imagine not being hungry. No one could remember when he had not been hungry. Building cities, plowing the earth, exploring the land, working in metal, engineering new roads, bridges, houses, writing poetry and plays, all the activity of intelligence embodied, imaginative, innovating— it all stopped. There was no more energy or love, no free play of will, no excess. They conjured, like feverish castaways, the most outrageous fantasies about food, things for which there was no name; globular, living, reddish, oozing, worlds of pip and juice, held out in the hand or on a swaying bough, making the tongue shudder in sensual delight! Imagine! Imagine! They grew mad with torment, they dreamed of the unheard, the unseen, the unimaginable.

And so they imagined themselves anew, men with tongues and taste and nerve ends, their beings fibrillating with ecstasy.

Then they came to their senses, of course. Clicking eyelids, clanking limbs, the whole monstrous race in motion, wary, circling one another, waiting for a kill, the moment when one of them, maimed or petering out, offered an opening.

In time, there were less of them. And less of them. And less of them.

They had pulled the world down about them. But what world?

It is told in the old myths; in the year they reached the moon, there were left on earth four species of quadrupeds: the hyena, the giant rat, the mole, and the armadillo.

The year they astonished the universe by a Mars landing, there was no single bird left on earth, save for a few domestic fowl, and a single disconsolate pair of white herons in the London aviary. Still there was compensation. The New York Public Library had a world-renowned collection of some fifty thousand bird calls on tape. These were broadcast on demand, which was not heavy.

By the time they achieved indefinite plasticized organic extension of human life, the Great Lakes were polluted beyond repair. Still, a man who so chose could now live beyond two hundred years, his brain and organs totally replaced by an external system. He could also see, on special video broadcasts wrap-around fidelity-colored movies of the Great Lakes washing about his hospital walls, the sound of waves all but drowning out the click and gurgle of the liquids driven through his shelf of plastic organs.

To be sure, the creation of the individual purafilter had been a race with time. For some 290 days, an air envelope from New York to Los Angeles had dumped on the land a lethal fallout of pollutants. But there had been sufficient warning—for most. By the time fifty days had passed with no relief, the survivors, all but some two million citizens, were fitted with plasticine globes over their heads. Each man could now set in motion a simple apparatus that assured him a flow of ready-mix air.

The globe could also be fitted, if one preferred optional equipment, with speakers and listening devices. Only a few could afford these, and even among those who could, such things eventually fell into disuse.

The contribution of that century was twofold. The plastic globe became in time a parabiological necessity, riveted to the shoulder bone in a surgical operation performed shortly after birth. Then, since the use of transistorized equipment diminished, so did language. In time, no one heard or spoke any more. The tongue and ears became residual. Men took to signaling one another, like deep-sea divers, with their hands.

It was the first metatechnological breakthrough. Man, speechless in his plastic globe, his eyes peering out like a fish's from a blue bowl of oxygen, fed intravenously, old as Tithonus and older, plastically and periodically replaceable in all his parts, more and more progressively liberated from the world, which in any case was now raped and sterile—man, superman at last, strode into his future.